*Personal
Copy*

Personal Copy

Ray Gosling

Five Leaves Publications

www.fiveleaves.co.uk

Personal Copy

Published in 2010
by Five Leaves Publications
PO Box 8786, Nottingham NG1 9AW
www.fiveleaves.co.uk

Originally published by
Faber & Faber in 1980

© Ray Gosling, 1980, 2010

ISBN: 978 1 905512 98 0

Five Leaves is a member of Inpress
(www.inpressbooks.co.uk)
representing independent publishers

Trade distribution: Central

Typesetting and design:
Four Sheets Design and Print

Printed in Great Britain

Contents

Part 2 Battle for the slums

Introduction

This is the story about where I live. A fairly true story. It is downtown in a large city, and it doesn't really matter which. How I got there and was moved into social action — small politics.

The book is about me and my growing up, away from my parents and finding my way in the swinging sixties — those most radical and amazing times. Believing the world would be permissively wonderful, bountiful and beautiful and free. It's also about how I got involved in one place in our time, that has been changed as totally and physically as if a conqueror like Napoleon had laid it waste in a ten-year war to change the face of the earth where I live.

I was a people's leader and these are my memoirs of what happened. How I tried to influence. Who else tried and who succeeded. Now the back streets have gone from English life — was it worth it? Who I am is important to the story and so I begin with myself. And my generation.

The *oldest* fit and alert person I know is a lady of ninety-six. I went in one day. She said, how are you? I said, I'm sick. She said, I'll do you some warm milk. I snapped back, I don't like milk: I don't want any milk.

"Oh," she stopped in her tracks, and leant on her stick and stared at me, very seriously. "I know," she spat it out, "you live up Ay Know's Yard, Joe Awkward's eldest son."

Part 1

A great preamble into nothing

At lilac evening I walked with every muscle aching among the lights of 27th. and Welton in the Denver colored section, wishing I were a Negro, feeling that the best the white world had offered was not enough ecstasy for me, not enough life, joy, kicks, darkness, music, not enough night... I wished I were a Denver Mexican or even a poor overworked Jap, anything but what I was so drearily, a "white man" disillusioned.

Jack Kerouac, *The Subterraneans*

A very deep life

When I was young I was young and I did the crazy things. When I was young I also pledged, solemn inside myself, I would be somebody to the world. I would do something with my life. Now I am older than Jesus Christ when he died — and what have I done? I have not buried my talents in a field. I have strived to be a person; to do good things and have freedom for my own life.

There is a tradition when you're knocking up to forty years old to turn your coat, to turn against the ideals of your youth. I know that on bad days in the bronchitic winter, at home when times are hard, when I am tired with work my heart is not in, I can be heavy with broken dreams. I can curse that I've wasted my years. Curse that I should not have believed so seriously. I should just have had a good time and taken life as it comes. But on sunny days I still believe — and with conviction. I'm not ready to recant and speak any conversion to "seeing sense" or "being decent". I'll not deny my radical youth. I'll not put down as errors my teenage dreams. I've felt so strongly. I was so certain in the 1960s that the times were changing. I chucked away my father's painstaking, little-by-little, up-the-ladder struggle for betterment — I cast that out with the ferocity of a hooligan. For the big world I savaged my small town inheritance of darn and patch and make your own; of neighbourliness and the Friendly Society; of giving a part of your life to a charity, a part to a steady job, a part of your money to the savings tin of the building society. That was all and that was all too much.

Both my parents were Christian, but not inordinately so. I mean, they did not pray every night or talk frequently of Jesus. They just went to church sometimes, and not the parish church. They went to the best church in town: best music, best preaching — a fair bus ride away. Their Christianity was handed down to them by

13

their parents as a practical way of living that helped them practise the self reliance they needed. They were self improving, free thinking people. My father was a Nonconformist. They were self sufficient out of necessity and belief. Fresh cabbage was better and cheaper than frozen peas. We never had tea or coffee or orange juice at dinner time. From my mum we always had cabbage water: "Drink your greens' water, it's good for you to the last drop of goodness."

Anything my parents couldn't provide they bought from the Co-op. A man in a suit came out on Monday mornings, sat down in the living room for half an hour and took the order for ten bobs' worth of groceries from my mum. On Thursday, a lad would bring the groceries up on a bicycle — bacon and cheese, porridge and sultanas and the occasional slab of Iraqi dates, packed under British supervision. Our Co-operative Society share number was 13903 and we got 1/3d in the pound dividend on our purchases. The dividend was added up, once a year on dividend day. It was a tidy sum and what we did with it I have forgotten. I do remember we only ever bought what was necessary.

The idea of a consumer society was very foreign to my parents. The idea you could purchase at whim, because something looked nice or someone tells you so. The idea of credit was anathema. Life was productive, and that's how it should be. You provided for your needs, not your fancy. Work was necessary and of value, almost a virtue. My father worked in a garage. At home he took in watches to repair from neighbours, for extra money, and built himself a shed from old angle iron, motor car wrecks and perspex. He creosoted fences — and the loft was converted into a workshop to make and mend more things that would be useful. Soldered saucepans.

When I won the scholarship to the grammar school I was bought a new Raleigh bike. Until that time our bicycles were cannibalised from bits of old scrap bicycles. My father's was like that. A wheel off one, a frame off

14

another, and my father went to work on an old bike like that. He made things — electrical things, mechanical things — but when he came home from work his time was spent repairing or digging the garden and tending to the greens, and the strawberries and the blackberries, and the richness of that garden. Every kind of cabbage and he'd try to propagate new varieties. Grew a tobacco plant. Though he didn't smoke, the idea was exciting. He tried to cure the leaves in the shed. Hours of wasted time. I remember the flowers only opened at night and gave off a beautiful, strange scent, powerful and eerie: the tobacco plant was very strange. I remember we had a strawberry bush and that he tried to get gooseberries without thorns on the stems, and then tried a hairless gooseberry. When night came, he'd go into the shed where he'd rigged up his own lighting from car batteries and work, at a bench, making things. Many of the things were things that we needed in the house, but others would be for the pleasure of the children and his own experimentation. Busy from morning to night. And so was my mother. That's how I remember things. That's how I want to remember things. I know my parents have come along with the times and today they too use teabags and have a little telly. They're not as young as they were. They put their feet up more and I'm not criticising anybody. I'm only pointing out the way times have changed, and how we all let them change.

I want you to understand I come from a good home, and I am fond of my parents. My childhood was happy. In the summer the sun shone, and in winter there was lots of snow, as I remember. I spent all my childhood in one place, Northampton, a market and factory town surrounded by countryside. I remember the countryside — that within minutes' walk there were hedges, ditches, ponds and frogs. Rabbits ran zigzag across the stubbly fields. There were butterflies on the cabbages in our garden. On hot days ants would appear by the hundred out of pavement cracks and my mum would tell me to "pour this kettle of boiling water on those ants". My mother's people came from further in the country, a real village some miles from our town. I went to that village often in the holidays and it was lovely. Water came from a hand pump. There was a village pond with ducks on. My Uncle Will worked for the lord of the manor as a gardener and his cottage had an Elsan lavatory. The rest of the family worked on the land — farm labourers: peasants. I don't think they'd have liked to be called peasants. My mother had been the brightest girl at the village school so the lord and lady made her the teacher. She got qualified, and then obtained a position teaching away, in council schools on the industrial suburbs of London. On holiday at a Bernard Shaw festival in Malvern she met my father. They were both admirers of Shaw. My father was a serious reader although he only worked in a garage mending motorbikes. "*Only!* — what's wrong with that? There's nothing wrong with work;" I can hear my mother correcting me, "if somebody didn't do it the world wouldn't get you very far." I often describe myself as a working class boy, but my parents wouldn't give thank you for that. They were working people, and not rich in material things. They had minds that thought independently, but they were poor. My father's hands were and are hard and grained with grease and dirt. Metal splinters had to be gouged out with a needle. Scrub them and there'd still be black beneath his fingernails, in the lines of his palms. He'd sing around the house: "I am the poor one, the poor one, the poor one."

Our house was a modern semi-detached, one of many built on the very edge of town in 1938. Bought with a fiver down and £490 to pay off at 12/1*d* a week for twenty-five years. Rates were 2/2*d* a week. Dad earned a basic of £2.10*s* a week, sometimes a bit more, but never came home with more than £3, and that was their only income. In the war he was in the electrical and mechanical engineers. There was a cornfield at the bottom of our garden, a hedge of blackbird nests, a ditch, a row of trees alternating lime and elm and then a farmer's field of golden corn, until the farmer sold it for a council house estate.

We didn't have an inside "loo". When did that word come in? Where you went to "do your business" was called the lavatory then. After the war some people began to put lavatories inside, but we wouldn't. We were the last, partly because we genuinely couldn't afford it, and also because my father said it was unclean to have a lavatory inside. Because of the smells. It was best to have the lavatory outside — but very cold in the winter. The pipes were lagged with old woollen vests and a paraffin stove was lit to take off the frost. The bedrooms were also very cold. Ice trees on the windows. You brought your own stone hot water bottle and we all got chilblains and rubbed some green ointment on to swollen toes. It smelt lovely. Winter green.

There were terrible fogs, when country boys were sent home from school at dinner time and in the evening the town buses were led by a conductress who walked in front of the bus with a screw top flashlamp. Our house was the bus terminus. One night I remember a conductress ringing our doorbell. Her bus driver had tried to, or had assaulted her and could she stay at our house for the night? Oh dear — of course she couldn't. It wouldn't be right. My parents were not getting involved. She must go home/report it to the proper authorities. Was not there a bus inspector?

We didn't have social callers. There was enough to do: "I haven't got time to gossip all day," they both said, often. There were no neighbours popping in, though they were always civil — "Nice day!" — over the garden fence. Everyone had high fences, the builder built them to enclose the gardens. There was so much to do, digging and planting and pruning. We never ate any fruit or vegetables but what we grew ourselves. Fruit and jam, chutney, bottled kidney beans, kilner jars of raspberries. There was fresh mint for the lamb, picked after church. Herbs of all sorts but no garlic. I mean, I never had chips

17

until I was fourteen or fifteen and went out on my own to a Greek café full of American soldiers at the bottom of Bridge Street. I ate the chips on a cheesecloth, chequered pattern tablecloth, with an old jukebox in the corner where we'd drop a twelve sided threepenny bit and a record would plunk on a platter and play, very scratchily: "I left my true love on blueberry hill..."

There were fish and chip shops near us but we cooked our own food. Food at home would be boiled or steamed in the kitchen. Washing up was done with soda crystals. On Mondays a great copper would be on the go, lit by gas underneath, for boiling clothes. Not a copper copper, but a greyish metal copper. Cabbage, potatoes and clothes, and a wooden copper stick gone mushy with the heat. The kitchen would be full of steam while my mother watched the clock and cut the Sunday joint: Monday cold, Tuesday minced with a mincer that had to be put together like heavy Meccano and, vice-like, screwed on to the kitchen table. If it had been fine my mother would put the washing out, mangling it through a great iron mangle and hanging it on the line. There was always washing on the line. That had to be taken in as soon as it started to spot. And then it would be hung on a wooden clothes horse in front of the fire, so we rarely saw the coal fire. The clothes horse was always there. Darning, patching and mending. If there was time, there would be a treat in the middle of the morning. Coffee — bought in a quarter pound bag, not at the Co-op but at a fine grocer's that reeked of coffee on the market square. I loved to stand in front of that grocer's and sniff. The grinder's vent gave directly on to the street. Ground coffee blown out. I'd sniff. Gosh, it was a superb smell. Gone like the fogs and frogs and steaming kitchens. My mother would make coffee, ground coffee grains and hot water in a jug not a percolator. Saucer over the jug. Let it settle. Then pour into cracked cups specially kept for coffee so they smelt of coffee even when washed and empty and hung on the kitchen hooks. Just one cup, weak but real and a piece of home made biscuit, fudge or cake.

My father would come home every day for dinner. Main course, followed by stewed fruit/rhubarb/apples/ blackberries with cold custard. No soup. No tea. Greens' water or water. The seasons were respected. Everything had its proper time and place. My mother grew a few snowdrops in the small front garden. In Lent we gave summat up and ate yellow fish on Fridays. No chocolate in Lent, and the hot cross bun was on Good Friday — not before. No one would have dreamt of eating an Easter egg before Easter. Not even I. In summer there would be the drought. We had it every year. We'd have no water in the tap but for an hour at sundown and I remember sometimes taking water with a bucket from a council cart, though we had our supply. My father had built a primitive water butt to collect rainwater. My mother — didn't she wash her hair in rainwater?

There were bike rides to a deserted village, its street overgrown with weeds, its houses and its church just left — the front door on one hinge still swung. Did it ever have glass in its windows? Left deserted since the Black Death or some such plague. The countryside was as close as a poem by John Clare — and twice as crazy. In September I'd be sent to the bus yard, for a letter had come from Uncle Will — he'd put a couple of shot birds on the bus. They dripped blood beneath the stairs. There'd be an awful lot of pheasant plucking and eventually a different taste and the alarming swallowing of lead pellets. Hare was skinned. Rabbit stewed. I remember Remembrance Day. At two minutes to eleven every bus stopped and all factory hooters sounded. The bus driver would get down from his cab, and stand beside it, cap in hand. The two minute silence — nothing moved on the street. Cyclists dismounted and stood bareheaded. Lest we forget. When the ice came, buses spun — I've seen them turn full circle. In the winter the river burst its banks, acres were flooded, and didn't we see cows in trees? At Christmas, we had a silver threepenny bit in the pudding but never any brandy.

19

We were happy. The whole street was a street in which people were buying their own homes, and everybody on the street was a working person, everybody went out to work. It wasn't middle class at all, and we didn't think we were one above anybody. Everybody just got on with working and they were all struggling to make ends meet. They were very proud and rather dull. Gas fitter, plumber, milk roundsman, a GPO switchboard girl who bought her house herself as a single girl. Next door was a bricklayer. The other side a plain factory operative. No one's light was ever on after midnight — after eleven. No one's curtains stayed closed after eight in the morning. Of course there were subtleties: gradations. For example, my mother was sure she wasn't like the townies. She'd respect and pride, in part, for the gentry of her village. My father's people had been deeply townies, and involved in politics, religion, and "goodness knows what", my mother would say. When the next door's cat was seen my father would rush to chase it with a rare display of temper. "You filthy hooliganism," he'd bawl, as he tore after the terrified creature with a spade and the poor moggy had to leap our extra high fence covered with thorny blackberry and loganberry brambles. He'd threaten to lay poison. "Not for nothing am I the nephew of a chemist. I do know about poisons: we've still got the formulas in the loft."

In fact it was sad. My grandfather, who I never met, had been the rising political star of the local Co-op, backstreet medicine, and goodness knows what. In those days, before my time, before the National Health Service, free medicine was possible if you belonged to a Friendly Society. My grandfather, a gardener in the town graveyard, had joined the Ancient Order of Foresters Friendly Society and stood for committee. He was elected and rose through elections to become full time paid secretary. They were only ordinary working men but they interviewed and appointed and paid for their own doctor and purchased their drugs directly. Today's working class communities may run their own boozing and darts and social club, but in those bad old days they appear to have had a real power the Welfare State has bureaucratised out of existence.

His wife, my grandmother, was elected on to committees of the Co-op and the Methodist church. She was still alive, a widow, and lived in a back street terraced house that was lit inside by gas — a two-up, two-down with very tiny rooms, which she made over warm and comfortable. To get by she made up wreaths and crosses in a small way. Her son, my father, had been bright at school but had to leave, his future thwarted when my grandfather died, suddenly before his time. And he left no money. Dad had to get a job and keep the family. But he inherited books and that was special.

In our house there were a lot of books. My mother had collected books in her youth, also my father developed his own strong tastes in literature: O. Henry, Wilde, Shaw, and a Methodist preacher, Stuttart Kennedy, was his hero. Religion and politics were talked about. Palmistry, too — he'd read the bumps on your head. Monologues my father recited at church firesides. *The Lion and Albert* by Marriott Edgar about a boring trip to Blackpool that a Mr and Mrs Ramsbottom made with Albert their son, a grand little lad, quite a swell.

> *They didn't think much to the ocean,*
> *The waves they war fiddlin' and small,*
> *There were no wrecks and nobody drownded;*
> *Fact nothing to laugh at at all.*

So seeking further amusement they went to the Tower Zoo where Albert poked a lion with a stick. He got ate.

There was Shakespeare, bound and read, several Bibles and Concordia (unread) but the books that governed daily life were in the living room: Newnes's *Everything Within,* Mrs Beeton's cookery book and *Pictorial Knowledge* bought for me on an instalment plan... and a *Daily Express* Home Doctor. Bandages were made up. We didn't buy Band Aids. My father's shirt tails would be cut and made to renovate/rejuvenate fraying collars and cuffs. My mother was always darning and patching and mending, sewing tails to collars, strengthening sock heels with old wool. I learned to knit when I was eight or so. I was taught how to knit dishcloths. I mean we never thought of going out to buy a dishcloth. You knitted dishcloths. Mine were very knotty and I never progressed. I had home knitted vests but my mother knitted these. We did things ourselves. Because — that was all we could afford. Because it was so. Because it was best.

My parents were not exceptional on the street. Their life was an improvement on the back streets and peasant cottages of their parents. Everyone went to work on a bicycle — tingaling ting — tingaling ting — "Good morning, Mr Gosling." "Good morning, Mr Hart." Tingaling ting. A way of greeting gone. A street cry that lasted for not as long as the old gypsy tatler's "any old rag 'n' bone." But longer than the tinker's scissors grinders on a bicycle. They're gone. We used them. Almost everybody had an allotment garden. Shears to be sharpened. Almost no-one had a privet hedge. Gardens were for produce. Almost no-one had a full lawn. For a long time, there was no sitting out in our garden. That garden was a working patch and it was a dig for victory — stamping on slugs, pulling up weeds, collecting droppings from the baker's horse, making compost of fallen leaves — a dig for survival.

With money they made sure that the children had the chances they'd had to forego. The children — myself and my sister — were very important to Mum and Dad and they did everything for the children. For the future my parents sent me to ballet class and elocution lessons. The Co-op dividend helped to pay. I was entered for Eisteddfod at Carnegie Hall. "Little Trotty Wagtail" was the set piece, by John Claro.

Little trotty wagtail, he waddled in the mud,
And left his little footmarks trample where he would.
He waddled in the water pudge and waggle went his tail
And chirruped up his wings to dry upon the garden rail...

I can't remember if I enjoyed it. I won no prizes but I went and to violin and piano lessons — my hands so cold, or black from changing the bicycle chain, or even worse all rubberoid from having to mend a puncture. I'd spend half the lessons with my fingers in a bowl of warm water. Private teachers doing tuition in their front rooms. Backstreet studios. Small town academies. Classes that had to be paid for by my mother and father. It's strange looking back, and trying to remember, because of the richness that was there. I mean, my mother's shoes were handmade — maybe this is because it was a boot-and-shoe town, with a large number of freelance craftsmen, but my mother had handmade shoes. My father mended them on his own last on the stone kitchen floor. My own first suit, at the age of six, was handmade by a little Jewish tailor in a back alley off Lady's Lane. My mother's sewing machine was mechanical: hand turning. She wasn't a middle class lady, she was the wife of a working man. And the wives, very few of them went out to work. They didn't have *time* to go out to work.

I don't think my parents were Victorian at all. Not at all. They were believers in the modern world. They were believers in science, hygiene, in engineering, and the better future. Maybe they were Victorian. I don't remember any feeling that we were entering the affluent society. It was simply that if we worked hard, if we made sacrifices, a better world would come. Better materially — spiritually — but was it ever spelt out like that? If the parents sacrificed, the children could enter the promised land.

We had a hard life but there were treats. My father's homemade sweets — gooey coconut ice, marbled fudge and luscious menthol delight. And once a week we were taken out for afternoon tea to a café in town called the Wedgwood. If we were lucky, and if we'd been good. We'd be shown in by the manageress and sat at a table laid for four, and waited on by waitresses in trim black skirts, pleated white blouses with little black caps and white pinnies. Sometimes my mother knew the waitress from the bus or church or our street. We'd have to keep our hands off the tablecloth and a fidget would prompt: "Don't you dare put your elbows on the table." We were allowed one cake from the cakestand. We never ate out for a meal. Proper tea was cooked at home later. Something more substantial: ham, egg and beans on toast. Cooked meals were at home. Afternoon tea was for tea and little more than plain bread, butter, jam and this one professional tasty cake. "And can we have some more hot water, please." Sweet tooth but it was a treat, and a parental exercise in how to behave in public: manners maketh man. Don't pick your nose. Lift your cup with the saucer. Don't slurp your tea or you won't get another cup. Don't you dare make that noise or we'll never come here again.

We had our holidays away — in a boarding house at Hunstanton, and staying with an auntie at Portsmouth. I can remember going to the Isle of Wight for the day and, when we got on to the boat at Portsmouth harbour, in the mud of the harbour there were poor children, urchins, begging for pennies like the boys who tout the motorway south of Naples today. Outstretched arms banging chests. Pointing fingers. It was the first time I saw anyone that poor. "We are the poor ones," my father would sing loudly as he banged about the house, but there were another poor. I knew I was lucky to have a good home. There was a street of poverty in our town. It was called Scarletwell Street. I never went there.

We were the last to get an inside lavatory on our road and the last to get a television. We had a radio, medium wave only, permanently tuned to the Home Service, switched on for the news and off at the end of the news: "That's enough." We didn't have the telly but the Dewises did. They lived in a road of slightly larger semi-detached houses with bow windows and garage space. They played in our garden, and I played in theirs — and then they got the telly, and on Saturday mornings I'd be invited into their front room for *Dunking Doughnuts,* a television show in which we audience at home were encouraged to dunk doughnuts in our coffee or our tea in time to the people doing it on television. The coffee and doughnuts, or bought biscuits, Mrs Dewis supplied. They were very kind and jolly and they had a carpet with a pile to it. Not like ours. I liked the Dewises but I was conscious they were better off. Mr Dewis was a foreman at a tannery and I think I remember he went there on a bicycle. Maybe his was a bought-from-a-shop bike — with splashguards!

There were larger houses — a distance away. Detached. Up drives. Secretive. Not a part of my world. If they had money, which they presumably had, they didn't seem to have much to show for it, it didn't seem to do them much good.

The Americans

The Americans were something else. I don't think they could ride bikes. Their bodies seemed different — bigger and broader beamed, and they walked with such a swagger: how would they ride a bike? Our town was surrounded by American Air Force bases. I can remember as a child going into the market square, and the long coaches would come in and the Yanks would stand at the top of the coach steps and throw chewing gum and Hershey Bars into the square, and, as kids do, we'd grab them. We were very much influenced by America and the Americans. When my father was out of the way in the loft, I'd try and tune our radio to AFN Frankfurt and listen to Jo Stafford. There was a tremendous romance about America. America was the place where we all wanted to be. America was closer to us than London.

The Americans had affluence: a roll of banknote readies stuffed in a back pocket. So casual. So available. And for a girl in our town who wanted class and flourish, the thing to do was wed a Yank, marry a GI. That was *the* way out. There was no other way out.

The Americans were there. I don't think I ever wondered why they were there. This was before Ban the Bomb and the Campaigns for Nuclear Disarmament got going. We didn't think about that. The Americans were just there. And one of them came next door to our house, and ran away with the nice next-door neighbour's wife. Just like that. A bolt from the blue. And the GI carried her back, just like that, to I think it was Wyoming. The poor husband had no idea. He came home from work and found a note on the kitchen table, and came across to my mum and said: "My wife's left me... Gone off with a Yank... and left me a note." That was how we saw the Americans. They could do things — just like that. They were like creatures from another planet. They had a

26

different way of life. They weren't the kind of people my mother and father had anything to do with. They were very attractive to me, though. They *looked* good. Some of them had big cars and when I was fourteen, fifteen, and, began to go into the town at night and walk around the streets, I used to simply follow them. The most exciting thing about being alive was looking at Americans. America was the dream, to go to America. Be like them. Maybe, if we were lucky, when they left they'd take us back to their promised land with them. Like the next-door neighbour's wife.

They were ambassadors for dreams come true, though they didn't mock or run us down as I remember. Indeed they called us "sir" and made a little bow; they were loud but polite. They spoke English but they really advertised themselves. They were flash and the real live Americans were more spectacular even than they were in the films. The amount of braggery that went on amongst them, the way they stood, their way with language, the fact that they swore, the fact that they were openly, affectionately kind and touching to one another, that they would talk to me, a child, as if I was an adult. Americans never talked down to me. They talked straight. And they appeared to be open about everything they did. I can remember one saying to me, "Could you find me..." — I must have been in the second form at school — "Could you find me a prostitute? You know their quarters?" I mean, they were smashing. They were... life with a capital L. They were the great temptation, the thing to be aware of. And I fell for this first temptation, head over heels in love with their freedom and their dollar. I don't understand this, looking back, but I mean looking back from now, I see my parents' way of life as something absolutely admirable and full of goodness and strengths I should have followed and built upon. I can't rationally understand why I didn't. There's no reason at all that I can put my finger on. It's almost as if — and it wasn't just me, there were others as well — it's almost as if we were taken over by the devil.

And the devil was America. They were the first attraction that made me want to rebel — and then came rock 'n' roll. That sent me hell-bent to smash to smithereens everything my parents' generation had built. And I don't know why. If we had known what we were doing, I don't think we'd have done it. But we didn't know what we were doing. That was the attraction — an adventure into the unknown through the jukebox, loud music, sultry music, American music, the blues, Jo Stafford, jazz, honky-tonk women, the first music from people like the Platters, a touch of falsetto. And this was a very superficial kind of life. Whereas my parents lived a deep life, I threw up the deep life for the superficial.

Grammar school

I was a lucky boy to get an eleven-plus scholarship to a grammar school, and it was a very good school. Awful and ancient. There was a school song: "When Thomas Chipsey found this school in 1541..." They were very intent to have me participate in things that got up my nose, yet I enjoyed it when I was persuaded to be one of the three little maids from school in *The Mikado*. We were constantly reminded how lucky we were to be grammar grubs. The teaching was a mixture of old tradition and a looking forward into the wonders of science that would provide mankind with a rational progress into a brave new world. Technology would solve all things. Science had come to save us. Education and hygiene, mind over matter, reason over emotion. In my last year they turned what were the bike sheds into a three storey science block which later faltered, so I don't suppose science is quite so sacred today. The old Edwardian building still stands, where they taught us ancient Greek and Latin. I couldn't do the Greek, but the Latin has always come in handy. At the coronation of Queen Elizabeth II, there was an idea that a New Elizabethan Age of British supremacy was dawning. We never believed in it. I remember the great Brabazon aeroplane that was the biggest plane the world had ever seen. And it did fly — hats off to Lord Brabazon. It got about eighteen inches off the ground — maybe a little more but not much and not for long. It flopped. And didn't it go to a museum? That was the Brabazon — the first Great British thing I remember flopping after that great heralding. Looking back, the Brabazon seems a sort of forerunner of a whole host of Great British exaggerated things that were going to make the world abundant and marvellous and flopped. I enjoyed reading *Biggles* and seeing *The Dam Busters* — a film about brave RAF bombers flooding a German installation. I cried at its jingo, and hated myself for being so moved. It was nice to see British pride burst. I don't know why. It was a laugh to see the future fall flat on its face: a custard pie for the boffin. I remember shoe shops installed an X-ray device to take pictures of your feet, so your mummy didn't buy you shoes that crimped your toes. All the shoe shops got them. Only later did we learn they damaged your feet.

As I went on in school I got more and more out of tune with it, filled with a real hatred for its snobbery, and its assumption that we were leadership material. I hated the assumption of getting on, the duties of being a credit to the school. I wanted to do what the Americans did. They let themselves go. At home everything had to be controlled. My parents couldn't have brought us up with freedom and choice if they hadn't strict regulation over every hour of their lives. Every part of the garden was cultivated. I wanted what the Americans had — wide, open spaces, free style, liberated energy and ready cash. They stood for letting yourself go as deeply as my parents stood for their belief. But the Americans said go on your guts, it doesn't matter about books and tradition, go on what is inside you: do what you feel.

At the pictures

Those sons from tougher working class, backstreets and widowed mothers — they did very well academically. But rebels tended to be from the home owning, bit better off working class. That was where the rebels were. At home and at school we shouldn't read comics. Comics were destroyed with the exception of the *Eagle,* a Christian educational comic edited by a most modern clergyman that featured a comic strip of the journeys of St Paul in colour — and *Dan Dare*, space pilot of the future, with his base commander, Admiral Commodore Sir Lancelot Uppity who was for ever saying into his balloon: "Off you go. Dare, teach them their lesson in Venus, old chap, best of British... you'll need it." Kids will be kids. There were a lot of pranks pulled for a day school. Frogs blown up with straws until they burst. Flick knives sharpened. Boys' heads dipped in lavatory bowls. I'd a pal we pushed into a quagmire in a quarry. We watched. He sunk above his waist before we phoned the fire brigade. Fireworks through old ladies' letterboxes — every year. Throwing school caps in the hubs of moving bus wheels. Sitting on a bus, upstairs above the driver, until he has before him a particularly difficult manoeuvre and then a gang of you all together jump up and bang your feet down on top of his head. I was in the Boy Scouts and the choir. It was a very good church. Cassock and surplice, collar or ruff. Sung eucharist and summer camp: "Riding along on the crest of a wave".

There was a theatre in the town. The impresario, Paul Raymond, brought us *Peaches Page,* a delightful dish, with or without. And *Strip, Strip Hooray* and *Top Town Nudes...* if they moved, they'd be arrested. The police came in large numbers and stood at the back looking closely. The finale ended in a flash of darkness and then the stage would be reilluminated to show the nude tableau: "We have Marilyn from Mablethorpe who makes men's mouths melt." Not even a wink. We whooped and threw chewing gum: if we could only get the girl to twitch she'd be arrested. Nude tableau was not allowed to move. The tableau had to be strictly tableau. Mr Buchwalter, the German teacher, took us on Mondays. Tuesdays we'd go on our own. Wednesdays we went again with Mr Buchwalter who once introduced me to one of the girls backstage. One show really did close. A rat had crossed the boards as Peaches Page posed, and bless her when she saw the rat she simply screamed and fled. All the PC Plods swooped at once. The safety curtain came down, the New Theatre shut for the rest of the week and Peaches Page was in court in the morning. Aaah. Silly laws. Later on in Bohemia they got sillier. I remember a bevy of Manchester detectives raiding one of the first nightclubs I ever visited. At this time you could only drink after hours with food, and food meant a substantial meal. Not a Mars Bar. The detectives were saying: "Have you had your meal?... Open your mouth... Was it substantial?..." Oh sweetie pie.

There was always trouble in my schooldays at the pictures. I remember one week the Savoy showed a 3-D film, the latest scientific wonder where usherettes handed out cardboard glasses as you went in. You put them on and you couldn't see much. You took them off and you couldn't see anything but blots and blobs and blurs, like abstract painting, like discotheque lightshows are today — and the whole picture show was in uproar with laughter and hysterics. You went to the pictures to enjoy yourself and if you came out hoarse and wet as a rag, that was enjoyment. Films were fun at that time.

There was a second-rate chain of three fleapit cinemas, the Tivoli, the Ritz and the Plaza, owned by one East End Jewish family of three brothers. There was always one brother on the door, dressed up in evening clothes with a dicky bow tie, a fat cigar and a welcoming grin.

"Good evening and welcome to the Tivoli."

"Tin hut!" we'd shout back at him.

"You're barred. Miss Tomkins, don't sell these Teddy boys any tickets."

We didn't need a ticket. In those days anyone who had sideboards and did their hair with a quiff was called a Teddy boy, but we always got in after a bit of lip and schmutter and a promise to behave. They needed Teddy boys'/teenagers' money at the movies, as parents were staying at home to watch the burgeoning television.

It wasn't just a small thing, young people at the pictures: it was a mass movement — hundreds went to the Temperance Hall on a Sunday night. The idea of *being* there was more important than the actual film — I can hardly remember a single film we saw. The films were things that were put up for us to barrack at the entire time. At the Temp, one of you paid at the front box-office, while as many as could hung round the back alley waiting for the fire exit push-bar to be pushed. Then you'd rush in for free before the commissionaire came running down to stop you. Sometimes there'd be a chase through the dusty seats. It didn't matter what film was shown, the Temperance Hall was a riot from beginning to end. You went for the audience. The stars were in the seats. "Wopper's in tonight, be some fun." You'd look round — "Tank's wid his girl" — and you taunted and participated. You hooted through the westerns — getting a good pow-wow going in the pit. You wolf-whistled through the romances. Mimicked everything. Torches flashed, plenty of catcalls. And the police were sometimes called.

I remember one film that didn't get barracked was *Rebel Without a Cause* at the Essoldo — not at the Temperance Hall — and it had a tremendous effect on me. The music was not rock 'n' roll but modern jazz, the plaintive whine of the saxophone: a sophisticated blues. In the opening shot, the teenage star, James Dean, is lying down in the road, drunk, cuddling a teddy bear, caressing and billing and cooing to it — going *aar, aaarrrh,* until his voice mimics the siren on the cop car come to fetch him, wow, wow, wow.

We didn't have sirens on our police cars then. Ours were black Wolseleys with bells, and in our films they were forever turning into Scotland Yard to be followed by Edgar Lustgarten in close-up, sitting at a desk, grimly telling us that in due time, according to the process of law, the guilty paid his penalty and was hanged by the neck until he was dead.

Rebel Without a Cause was a real film — and a lot of us said "Hush" when anyone tried to barrack it. It was watched in an unusual and rather disturbing embarrassment. I saw it three nights running and it had a lasting effect on me. The story of a sensitive boy, lean, meaningful and broody, breaking from his parents and trying to find and feel his own life. And we knew the actor James Dean, alive in the film, was dead in real life. It made it all "religious". And then a film came called *Blackboard Jungle,* a cheap film at a cheap cinema about a high school in America where the teenagers beat the teachers up. There was one good teacher and he, I think, was black: the rest were bullies — anyway it was a jolly good boo, clap and foot-stamping film. It was in *Blackboard Jungle* that we first heard the song "Rock Around the Clock" — just the song — which was the theme music of the film.

> *When the clock strikes 1, 2 and 3,*
> *we're going to rock, rock, rock,*
> *till broad daylight*

It was like an electric shock, and we all just stood on our chairs and in the aisles and howled. We went bananas at the screen.

It seemed that one moment, there I was, a Wolf Cub in short trousers, putting two fingers to me forehead and repeat after me, dib dib dib dib, I promise to do me best, to serve my God and King, to serve my God and King, and do a good turn to somebody every day, and believing it.

34

One moment I was collecting stamps of the British Empire, and being taken to the Dome of Discovery at the Festival of Britain and seeing with pride a great future of British adventure and science where man would come into his inheritance throughout the Empire. And the next moment in life I was drinking black-and-tans in the Criterion or the Horse and Groom and looking up at Johnny Facer open his flick knife and say, "Johnny Ray singing 'Crying in the Rain' — that's women's music, don't play it — right? — from now we've banned it."

One moment I was a privileged grammar schoolboy, lined up with all the other boys on the tennis courts, and the Combined Cadet Force presented arms as accompanied by the headmaster some dignitary gave each boy a firmly shaken hand and a gilt bound copy of *The New Elizabethan Age* by Richard Dimbleby.

And the next moment I was in the woods — with the rebel grammar grubs, just a few of us below the rugger fields. When we should have been playing cricket, we were drinking cider from the bottle, smoking Turf cigarettes, and practising curling our upper lips. I think we curled our lips up before we saw Elvis Presley do it on the cinema screen. We'd practise how to walk leery without being a nance — and we'd part one another's hair at the back into a style called the Duck's Arse.

One moment I was a choirboy singing "Jesu, Joy of Man's Desiring", and the next moment it seemed I was running in my luminous socks from an affray at the Cow Meadow Fair, bawling through the streets up to the bus station: "Hail, hail rock 'n' roll, deliver me from days of old." They always played rock 'n' roll records at the fair, fast, to speed up the rides.

I don't remember *seeing* the film *Rock Around the Clock* the first time, but I was there, in the cinema, taking part in the outrageous behaviour. Being at the time a fairly intelligent grammar schoolboy, I also remember all the fuss in the newspapers: reports of Teddy boys running riot in cinemas, seats being slashed, and the police being called to stop jiving in the aisles to the music of the devil, that's what they said. I was outraged, and I wrote a letter to *The Times*.

In our school we took *The Times* newspaper in the library, and there had been some correspondence on the subject of Teddy boys. The correspondence was roughly speaking between two parties. There were those on the one hand who wrote to say rock 'n' roll was the music of the devil, a degenerate cacophony that would destroy the moral fibre of our young people and put the future of the nation in peril. Didn't the Roman Empire decline through just such decadence? This rock 'n' roll would unsettle people and the Russians who had banned rock 'n' roll were quite right and we should do the same. The other party who wrote to *The Times* said it was much ado about nothing, rock 'n' roll, isn't it only young people letting off steam? Harmless music, rubbishy maybe, but a fad that would pass, a flash in the pan, and in fact Teddy boys, aren't they rather attractive and colourful, when they're clean? — young manhood regains his peacock feather. There was a book *Peacock's Tail...* This rock 'n' roll is only becoming serious because people are treating it seriously. Didn't we all participate in some kind of outrageous behaviour when we were young — bright young things and flappers. Of course so many youth today have nothing to do, said some correspondents. Society should certainly provide more for young people, amenities like youth clubs, and the Duke of Edinburgh, the Queen's husband, set an example.

Both parties made me cross. It wasn't what I felt at all, so I wrote my first letter to *The Times* — and I wrote it secretly for both the grammar swots and the followers of fashion in the school would have mocked me if they'd known. I wrote more or less saying that rock 'n' roll is not a passing show, you just wait and see. Rock 'n' roll is here to stay. It's music and it's more than music — it's a serious, outward and visible sign of a revolutionary change in the hearts of young people everywhere who are demanding the world be theirs. Rock 'n' roll is smashing and it's going to smash all the fuddy duddy civilisation to smithereens. Rock 'n' roll will change the world — signed a Teddy boy.

Maybe if I'd signed it a grammar schoolboy me letter would have been published. Not that I ever was a Teddy boy, exactly, not really, but I looked up to Johnny Facer, the King of the Teds in our town, and he'd let me be with him. I ran with the younger lot sometimes at weekends, down the main street, the rabbit run. We'd go from the billiard hall to Lynn's caff, the only caff with a jukebox, and from Lynn's caff to the billiard hall back again. In our little luminous ankle socks — mine were green luminous socks — and my first shoes were dark navy blue suede: brothel creepers they were called. They squelched as you staggered down the street, slovenly sloping your shoulders, and moving your pelvis, and curling up your lips: a lumbering, lumpen gang of yobs — and gosh the shoppers would stare, and stand apart and draw in their breath. It was like being with Moses parting the Red Sea when we walked down the Saturday streets, and that was marvellous. My second pair of shoes were winkle pickers — silver buckle and eight-inch-long pointed toes. Of course my parents knew I'd got them but they didn't know what I was doing. "Just going out —"

"Again! In those!"

On Sundays we hung around the bus station filing our nails with long metal nail-files, conspicuously leering at people, daring them to stare you back. If ever they did, you were supposed to bowl across to them, and say slowly: "Wor you looking at then — eh?" Nothing, nothing, they'd say, averting all but the corners of their eyes. If you were a fit Ted you might add another sentence — as the victim backed away you'd say: "You'd better half not be mate. If I catch you looking again, me and the boys'll come — do you over. We're not to be looked at. You look anymore, waphead, and you'll have to be taught a lesson." But I was never brave enough to add such a second sentence, nor would any of the boys have backed me up. I was just around.

When the film *Rock Around the Clock* came, everybody went. It seemed our whole generation stood in the cinema aisles, bawling back at the screen the choruses of those songs: "Razzle Dazzle" shouted Bill Haley, the star of the film. "Razzle Dazzle", we all hollered back. "Giddy up a ding dong" — or was that from a later film? There were so many. "See ya later alligator" — that was *Rock Around the Clock* surely — "At a while crocodile."

Remember these were the days before soccer had hooligans. There was no chanting; on the football terraces it was "Up the cobblers!" and "Well done Stanley Matthews." It was at the cinema we bawled our heads off, "Shake rattle and roll" was just what we needed. As if possessed by the devil, and the fit Teds did handstands in the aisles.

The film caused a national sensation. The Blackburn Watch Committee banned it. At the Trocadero, Elephant and Castle, hundred strong mobs of Teds came raving out of the cinema berserk, driven crazy and went on the rampage in the streets. At Croydon the police were called to fighting inside the cinema, but when it came to our town, the police were surely there at the back, and bouncers at the front, but I remember no aggro — it was just *the* experience of our lives.

The storyline was awful corny, a bit of a let down after all the ballyhoo; it made me squirm however good the music. And Bill Haley was no star we could identify with, no sulky, sultry Marion Brando or James Dean, not a fit youth but an old man, fortyish, who looked a square in his checked shirts with what was called a kiss curl across a balding forehead and this permanent gormless grin. But it didn't matter. The words and music mattered, and they were something else.

The story was about this country singer, Bill Haley, and his band, the Comets, who played at a local hop. The kids are enjoying the music when one day this big agent-promoter rides by and, after seeing how the music "sends" people, signs the band up, and books them for the big city and television. The adults/viewers are affronted and outraged. But "I'm just a country boy," says kiss curl Haley, "I am no Frankenstein." The Big Man works on the mayor to stop the band getting banned — they do good deeds for a day and turns for charity to prove portly Bill Haley really is a regular guy. He sings one song with a melody. You see, isn't it just all good clean fun!

Those words: "Let's rip it up, we're gonna rip it up at the joint tonight", which taken literally had put fear up the spines of the elders, were just slang for doing what comes naturally — having a good time. No-one was really going to rip it up or hurt anyone. And we close with Grandma and the Chief of Police doing a hand jive in the kitchen, sneaky smiles all over their crinkled faces. I thought what a cop out, and that's been the history of rock music ever since. A constant battle with the businessman saying it's just good fun, and the kids trying to say something with the music, to give the lie to Tin Pan Alley packaging; a deep feeling into just another merchandise. Whenever I heard — and the scene appeared in almost all rock films — the big agent-promoter explain it all to the mayor, I thought what a cop out. That agent-promoter is telling a lie. I never felt rock 'n' roll was just good fun. I suppose some people did — cretinous clerks and Teds from the villages might have thought rock 'n' roll was just a new game to play like skipping rope and spinning top, but I was a grammar grub and I knew the world was changing. Let the good times roll, live for the day and forget about school and books — and when everyone stood up and stomped through *Rock Around the Clock,* that was it. The first public demonstration of how our generation felt against our parents' world. No more aping adults. No more dressing like dolls. We were standing up and saying we've arrived: the first of a new tribe — the teenagers — and the world from henceforth was to fear and be enthralled by youth. The clock had started for our time had come. I really thought it was the beginning of a revolution and rock 'n' roll was the trigger: something I have always found difficult, or embarrassing, to admit. Although books and pictures were important, what triggered me off more than anything else was the jukebox. When it thumped, my heart uplifted. Out on the streets. Class warfare. Saturday night's a good night for fighting. Making whoopee. Nothing like a good rampage.

Rock 'n' roll was never a safety valve for me but a clarion call. And when the 1960s swung it wasn't a mere fashion, the swing of the social pendulum to permanent licentiousness — it was always much bigger than its commercial exploitation. It trumpeted the dawn of a Golden Age — of freedom, liberation, of leisure and pleasure — more to do with personal liberation than political economy. But it was political. And religious. And sexual. As when jungle drums beat for war, I wanted to rise up when I heard the jukebox cacophony, guitar twang. It was in the actual beat of the music. And then when Elvis leered, stood still and then gave that twitch... that was... What was it? I don't know in my mind. I know I felt strongly, where my father thought carefully. I assumed the best of strangers, where my father took nothing on chance. I threw myself against "them" because Momma don't allow no rock 'n' roll in here, so I broke from my whole upbringing of provident, prudent folk. My parents were so good and kind but their standards had to be overthrown, and with venom, if I was to be certain I was free. Baby out with the bath water.

Of course there were more influences than rock 'n' roll. Films like *Rebel Without a Cause* and the one film that did get banned in Britain, *The Wild Ones* with Marlon Brando. But the poster for that film was in circulation, and just that poster was exciting and moved me. There were books, a series of cheap books I remember for the lurid covers of boys in blue jeans and bomber jackets moodily leaning on lamp-posts: they were by Hal Ellson and *Reefer Boy* was one title I remember. There were new wave English writers; I never read any *Lucky Jim* stuff

40

but I knew it was around and I liked the title of Colin Wilson's *The Outsider* though I've never wanted to read it. Jack Kerouac's On *the Road* about the beat generation I did read. I went to see John Osborne's play *Look Back in Anger*. I was aware of economists talking about a consumer society and an emergent teenage market. I knew immigrants were arriving in numbers to make England half-English, to borrow a phrase of Colin MacInnes'. Moralists worried about the loosening permissive morality. There were even stories in newspapers that made a strong impression. One in *Picture Post* I fondly remember was pinned on my bedroom wall for a long time. It was illustrated with superb black and white photographs of ordinary lads looking romantically rough. The story was by Trevor Philpott about some curate or minister of religion who had organised a trip for this bunch of Liverpool lads. They went to London for the day, an outing in a Dormobile. The vicar drove. It was to be their real treat of a lifetime: for they'd never been to "the Smoke" before. They parked in a street in Willesden, and to the curate's amazement the youths sat in the van and played pontoon, poker or some card game for twelve hours. That was all they did. Never left the van — except I suppose for a wazz. The curate and Mr Philpott, the reporter, were amazed and shocked. They couldn't understand. I thought it was terrific. What style! I cut it out and stuck it on the wall.

Rock 'n' roll was the understanding, the release that got you off your seat and churned you upside down. It also enabled you to do nothing. Roaring down to Brighton and doing nothing when you get there. Leisure meant loafing. We slept a lot. We used to drink. There would be a day of drinking with boring abandon. Black-and-tan. Vile concoctions. Playing skittles without smiling or speaking and then great oathing at one another. Two of you face each other in the street and oath like billyo. Make a real exhibition and then carry on walking down the street as if nothing had happened, parting the crowds. We'd drink and smoke: smoke without removing it from your mouth. Down drink with the lower lip. Fag dangle on the upper. Make it rise like a penis. And get very drunk. Cider and Guinness. Stupid mixtures. Like getting hold of something and shaking it and holding on to it like a dog with a bone to the grim and mushy marrow end.

Absolutely drunk, we'd go into a Greek café, then have a meal. And the object was to eat and eat as much as you could, and then puke up. Everybody. I mean nobody... nobody enjoyed it at all and the whole point of it was to be unhappy. When I say we didn't enjoy our meals in the caffs, we didn't — the food was immaterial. I suppose the thing we enjoyed most was (it sounds daft saying this, but it's true), was the puking-up afterwards. My parents you see, had never seen life. That was my theory. I was living. Drinking to be sick: puke. Dancing on the billiard tables.

Teds hated the Americans. We had to be flasher than them and to let ourselves go more than them, and yet we used to do a large amount of loafing, where you would do nothing but act leery and loaf. I mean to stay in bed late... was perfectly all right. To stay in bed in your under-clothes and sweat. To just stand on a street corner. To go into a pub and do nothing but sit there. We couldn't do the get-up-and-go things the Americans could do. We hadn't the ackers... but we couldn't do it somehow if we had and so — this is looking back — we found a way of being ultra dreary. If the Americans were flash and kind, we'd be flash and unkind, and ghoulish and rude. We maunged about. Abaht.

Rock Around the Clock was shown in October 1956, and only months afterwards Radio Luxemburg was playing so many songs by young people. Youth had taken over, so it appeared. I went to London at weekends: changing in the train from my school blazer to my long blue jacket. I remember walking down East Street market in South London one Sunday. I mean I can remember what the weather was like and on the radio *Family Forces*

Favourites was playing a hit record with a catchy tune, not really rock but with a strong beat, called "Singing the Blues" by Guy Mitchell, a podgy-looking American singer from the photograph of him on the sheet music. But on the market stalls, the record trestles were playing the same song sung by Tommy Steele, and there was a croak in his voice like he meant the words, and there were photographs of him bulldog-clipped to the stalls and Tommy Steele looked like us — cheeky British youth with tousled hair and pouting lips and a Cockney so-fucking-what look. Couldn't care a toss. Then he made a film about himself becoming famous in the skiffle cellars of Soho. It was all right. *Rock with the Caveman.* A second film quickly followed and this was called *The Duke Wore Jeans* — everybody was doing it, chinless wonders rocking with champagne at the Savoy, the debutantes had taken it up. Tommy Steele was the darling of the upper classes. So quickly I got disillusioned. There was a Tommy Steele song hit called "Nairobi". We'd been fighting a colonial war with the Mau-Mau and I was on the Mau-Mau side, up the rebels wasn't the way rock 'n' roll was going. Its treatment by Tin Pan Alley was to have Teddy boys tidied up into teenagers. The young stars sang one good rock song and the next moment they were in pantomime and all round entertainment on the pier. Bill Haley came to this country in person. He came in like a lion and went out unnoticed. It was nothing: silly girls and reporters but the music was there. When Elvis Presley sang "All Shook Up", July 1957, we got that rush again. Elvis was terrific. When he sang "Turn Me Loose", that was the feeling, and he spat his songs and shook and murmured with the bottled up emotion we felt. When he twitched his leg and tossed his lanks we knew it was sex. Rock 'n' roll was a euphemism for sex, but not the girl next door. We wanted to fuck the world, and Elvis never really lost the sneer and swagger, the pent-up tremble, the fury of full throated rasps, but in time he was doing the novelty numbers — "There's No Room to Rhumba in a Sports Car" was a kind of American equivalent to pantomime. But let us never forget that when Elvis first appeared on television, they wouldn't let him be shown from the waist down.

Whenever the fair came, there'd be lots of Buddy Holly played fast to shorten the rides and increase the excitement. Good plain beat Buddy Holly who didn't look so pretty and kept it straight, and didn't go for pantomime and died so young. Like James Dean, he was to be forever evergreen. Gene Vincent was another real rocker who didn't compromise and a good mean-looker in black leather. He came over to Britain to a ravers' reception from the boys.

There was a smashing native singer, a really beautiful, mean and moody-looking boy called Terry Dene, rock star. I went to see him at De Montfort Hall and he sang a song called "White Sports Coat" — "A white sports coat and a pink carnation, I'm all dressed up for the ball" — like he'd had elocution lessons. The girls loved it and he threw his carnation to them for all the world like Noel Coward. It wasn't rock 'n' roll.

Larry Parnes was a famous agent out of London who set up in a farmhouse near Rugby a stable of youths he'd almost picked up off the streets. He'd have them groomed for stardom: golden boy heroes, stage studs — and he changed their names to call themselves Power, Pride, Fury, Wilde, Eager. British showbusiness began presenting boys. They were nice boys, said their agents. We knew how different, or did we? First there'd be a hard rock disc and a picture of them in a black jacket in the back streets of Liverpool, or sweating in a Soho coffee bar. Then, soon enough, this would be followed by a news story about their future as an all round entertainer. "But I'm not deserting my fans," quote, "who've helped me get where I am." The very successful ones had books published of their life story with the most creeping, toady quotations — this one is from *The Cliff Richard Story*...

> *If he hadn't been the Duke of Edinburgh, if he
> decided to be a pop singer, folks like Elvis and I
> would have been also rans.*

Another:

> *I don't mind betting that if I could go to Moscow,
> we'd soon be having these Russian kids doing the
> hand jive.*

Teddy boy back

In the beginning it was a battle to get your hair done. Most stylists or barbers, as they were called in those days, were men who'd been wounded in the war and they cut short back and sides with conviction — but in one fairly big salon, downtown, a barber called Wally began to specialise, in his corner, styling Teds' hair. Wally the hairstylist. He was in an ordinary barber's shop, Wally was, and on Saturday mornings, the owner used to let him mess about with Teds. And slowly the shop got taken over and then Wally got an apprentice called Reg, and the two of them used to do Teds, all the time then in their own salon. Teds made Wally. You used to go in with your hair filthy. You used to have it washed by Reg, and rubbed with a towel. Wally then approached you, wearing a different, rather natty, new-style barber's jacket like a dentist. He was a good cutter, serious and your front quiff he would curl with hot irons. You'd then be finished off under a drier with a hairnet on, feeling silly and cissy. Reg'd come and feel you. Wally'd give you a final blow, a last flick and it was beautiful when you went out. "I do like to see a Ted clean," said Wally and as soon as we were on the street we'd spoil it. We used to plaster it with coconut grease from Boots the Chemists: thick grease. I remember a cold day when it was freezing and I couldn't move my hair at all and had to get near a coke boiler to warm it up 'cause the grease had all frozen. Solid coconut grease. When it was hot weather it melted and ran down the back of your neck, spoiling your nice white shirt — but we wanted our hair to look greasy, not clean.

Dancing was difficult. The Palais and the Salon said no rock 'n' roll to begin with — we had to go up Drill Hall when a big band like Ted Heath or Eric Delaney played for a dance. Plenty of bouncers but they let us in: we were the attraction. We'd loll and mooch about, chewing gum and looking mean, until the band would eventually play "Razzle Dazzle" or something from *The Girl Can't Help It* and every Ted would be on the floor, suddenly. Sometimes there were fights and the band would change to a foxtrot tempo while we were being chucked out, and let's face it, that was no disgrace — being thrown out made your reputation. Then there was a local man who started booking the room above the Co-op down Far Cotton end of town and he began dance sessions to records every Tuesday and Thursday. He called it Ron's Gayeway at the Far Cotton Co-op and people did incredible dances — people let themselves go. There was drink there, it was teetotal, but real Coca Cola. People let themselves completely go but Ron had been in formation. He was a fanatic for steps and approached rock 'n' roll with a missionary zeal. Pretty quickly he was prettying it up, making you do steps in tempo and variations in rhythm — one, two, up and over your shoulder... Girls he wanted to wear pretty party dresses and he wouldn't let boys dance together.

I didn't have an ear-ring; some people had ear-rings. I didn't have any tattoos; some people had tattoos. But I had the hair. Oh silliness. And an outfit from Montague Burton. Because I was at grammar school I had to be a little careful, because of who my mother and father were and their standards. But the jacket was blue with a super silky, I think it was a red, lining and black trousers, very tight around the bottom of the trouser leg, round the ankle. What a tussle I had with the assistant. I could only just get them on. You'd choose the cloth from a swatch and then came the measuring — lower, really, sir, you'll look ridiculous. I said lower. Tighter — you won't get them on, sir. And sometimes I used to have to put Vaseline on my ankles to get them off. Or coconut grease. And then they were very baggy round the crutch, it wasn't at all like today's fashions. And I'm not sure M. Burton would have approved. He was Sir Keith Joseph's hero. A capitalist with heart. Above his every shop there was a ballet hall, and all the names of the stores in his empire he had emblazoned in gold on the black fascia — Paisley, Plymouth, Oxford Street. Across the road from Burton's was the Fifty Shilling Tailor — I can remember standing there and see them take down that sign — Fifty Shilling Tailor. But Burton had a kind of slogan, he wanted to see every man in England clothed in a suit like a bank clerk.

Burton's were good to me. You had to fight to get what you wanted but my blue jacket was lovely. It came down to just above my fingertips, and then I'd wear an ordinary white shirt — we used to turn the collar up at the back so it stuck above the jacket — and a silver necklace, plain necklace with a crucifix on. I had to send it back, the jacket, several times before it was right, but at the end of the day I was admired and afeared.

The Grubbies

Very, very few people that I've talked to and very few people I've ever read have grappled with the phenomenon of rock 'n' roll. It was nothing consciously to do with affluence. It was nothing to do with boredom. We didn't feel we were being manipulated by a leisure industry, or any larger force as left wing people thought. It wasn't a reaction to anything political. It was nothing consciously to do with the bomb which we, in our small town, surrounded as we were with American servicemen, were hardly conscious of. It was nothing to do with class. It was just this feeling... that we were important, that something was going to happen. How, in what direction, we didn't know. And we didn't much care. It was a very, very, very odd feeling but we felt it.

I was a Ted, not in the hard core. I was only a follower, part of a wave, but I was a believer. I was also in a group of working class grammar schoolboys christened the "grubbies" or "arty farties". We were interested in things of the mind. It was a rather elite set. None of them had Teddy boy interests and they pooh-poohed me a bit — though we were all moved by James Dean. One of these grubbies, his parents may have been a little deaf, lived in a flat which was unusual with a front room looking onto a main road. The room had a high ceiling. There was a record player with speakers, and his collection was classical. We used to sit there on the floor, sometimes in darkness, three or four of us grammar grubs and we'd play as loud as we could doom-laden Stravinsky and Vaughan Williams and read Thom Gunn and loving all the big boom. And a feeling that something was going to happen, the same feeling — that we were capable of changing the whole way the world was. Of changing our own life. A new world. If we'd been ten years later I think we would have been listening to the Pink Floyd with

49

heavy drugs and something would have happened. Maybe. Maybe. Anyway for us it was *The Rite of Spring* by Stravinsky. And we would just sit there, holding ourselves, posing to ourselves, some of us smoking, and let this huge sound sink into us. Doing nothing else. And coming out of the flat, I suppose emotionally disturbed — high — and going alone into the street and thinking that you were... a being... feeling a sort of loneliness and being glad that you were alone... that some force of nature would shape destiny for you as you breathed in. That's putting it too grand maybe... but you had the sense that something was... going to happen.

Never had it so good

Now how I got the money to spend time with the Teds was by working. My parents couldn't do any more than keep me in the bare essentials during term time. My father said, when I was fifteen, if you want to stay at school that's good, we're pleased and we'll help all we can — but for any money you want for yourself you'll have to earn your own pocket money. Since I was thirteen I'd done a paper round but that wasn't going to bring in enough even if I did it morning and night which I did. Other work was very casual. We had delivery boys bringing us things. I did it. Most did it. It wasn't an inferior class that was a delivery boy. I collected old newspapers, door to door, and pushed them down town in an old pram to the tatters' yard. It could be good money, and learning to bargain. Learning to experience the losing of a bargain. Too much stuff, and the old varmint doesn't want to take it. I don't want to wheel it back. Learning to reach a compromise.

I was always needing more money. My most ambitious idea was a job on the railways because I liked trains, and ran a loco-spotting club. I went down to the local station, and they didn't want temporary workers. Someone said there might be jobs on the railway some ten miles east, so I went over to the little iron town of Wellingborough to see the bloke who looked after signalling, from Leicestershire right down to Bedfordshire. After a lot of talk and fighting and persuading I got trained as a relief signalbox boy. These things were possible in those days. There were a lot of jobs, and I went back every long holiday for three years. The money, compared with other ideas and other people's luck, was simply fantastic. Once I'd learnt the ropes I'd be on a basic of about six pounds a week, and then there was overtime and Saturday afternoons and night work. They were very hard up for staff.

The boss who set me on was very kind. I can still remember his name, a real man, Mr Egan. He took a chance. It was a responsible job, and my first rubbing up against the working class. I was very young and sensitive. He was full of the glories of making nationalisation work, and the strengths of the men on the line. "I'm putting you in with Wisp first," he said. "I think you'll like Wispy. There's a lot of ill feeling among some of the men against Wispy, but I like him. I think you'll be all right. He stayed on, you see, after retiring age." I didn't see. I couldn't see how the men would go against him for that. "Young Porky'll train you. Bit rough with the language, but you won't mind that. They'll pull your leg a hell of a lot, but Ray, you just hang on tight." He called me by my Christian name. He looked me in the eye. "How will you get here for six?" I'll bike. I'll be here. I was: every long holiday.

Most mornings I got a lift on a baker's van, with my bike, but cycling home ten miles after a shift was a sweat. I began to understand what work was. The signalbox and all its works were amazing. Bells rang, and trains passed and Porky kept swearing down the telephone, and Wispy swearing at Porky. Talk about growing up. In my family there was absolutely no bad language — ever. At school and among the Teds there was but deliberately used to shock. In the signalbox there were vicious oaths and every second syllable was filth without reason. Porky would suddenly jump up, swing a lever across and jump back on his stool, and pick up another telephone and yell into that.

I learnt bell codes and books, telephone switchboards, and how slowly the last hour passed before your shift was relieved. Draughty, physically hard, pushing and pulling levers — this was before pushbutton electronic points and signalling came in. I began to understand what work is. How hard. How trapped. Turn around — six to two one week, two to ten next, and then a week of nights. Counting your rest days. Weighing your overtime. As a

52

junior I had to clean windows, whether they were clean or not, whatever the weather, with a leather and elbow grease and these were days when we wouldn't dream of wearing rubber gloves. We were men.

After Porky had trained me I was on my own with the signalman. It was one signalbox but there were three shifts, and my shifts overlapped. So I got to know three working people very well. One, Fred, was an ordinary jolly man — easy come, easy go, an optimist of little intelligence. Another was a very strict man. I think he was a bit like my father in fact. He was very precise about work, everything had to be done properly and he didn't have time for sociability. He was to some extent a gaffer's man. Thought no colleague did the work properly except him. A stickler for regulations. All three of them thought they were the best. They could never unite. They all bitched about one another. "What kind of mess has he left it in for me then?" The third man was Wisp, and he did sometimes leave things in a mess.

He was sixty-seven, two years over retiring age. This meant that some of the younger men who had hoped for his job when he retired were being done down out of the key job — the most prestigious signalbox and a few shillings more in pay. The thwarted ones tried every method they knew to unseat Wisp — in the Union, with the Inspectors, making his life more tough than it could possibly have been otherwise, and it was tough enough. Wisp, people said, was a communist, but he was a treat for me, and a temptation. He never insulted you without apologising. He was a thinking man, yet playful and devious as a cat — he could be alternately vicious, charming, and moody. He was the first man I ever met who was in all sincerity and honesty for the workers. He was a big bloke in the Trade Union and Labour. He had no formal education, but was a great reader of books and interested in ideas. He would bring his literature, from the *Soviet Weekly* to *Tribune,* to work with him. The men, even his enemies, would bring their Union dues and their

Union troubles to him. He was for strikes over wages. He was for large differentials. It was the time when ASLEF, the Locomen's Union, came out on strike to support the claim of top money for top men. Wisp wanted the signalmen to do the same. They were just as much key men as the loco lads. There was a great gulf at the time between the locomen and the running staff. Even Wisp was affected by it. Signalmen spitting at engine drivers.

He said — nationalisation, it's made it worse, lad. Before we had bosses. Now you don't know who your bosses are, and they does you down just the same. How can you have nationalisation in capitalist society? He explained the wages structure to me and these lessons from him drew me more than anything else into taking economics in the sixth form.

It took, still does, years as an ordinary signalman to reach Wisp's position. You had to sit exams, then work as a relief signalman when a regular man took sick. Then there were years of waiting for a permanent vacancy: for the man at the key box, the man like Wispy, to die or retire. If at any time you made one mistake you were downgraded, right back to porter it could be — and begin again. It was a lonely job, needing a great amount of personal discipline. Decisions had to be taken alone. The only contact was the telephone and bell signals. There wasn't always time to check. One mistake in our box and your fellow signalman down the line could be led into making a grave mistake, and every minute we could make mistakes that meant lives. You had to have the complete confidence of the other men on the line. It took nearly thirty years of hard graft to even join the waiting list for a key job like Wispy's, and if there was any blemish on your record the chances were very slim. The chance of a clean record was about equal to that of a lorry driver. And what did the key job entail? Easy shifts, good money, and an end to the hard graft? No, the shifts were the same as everyone else's, the graft twice as hard. It was the busiest box on the line for twenty miles either way.

Wisp was a communistic socialist and a Roman Catholic and he openly desired women. He used to stand at the window looking at every passing girl. He was a very deep and respectful "dirty minded" man. When I was on his shift at weekend nights he'd get quite emotional. We both did: moist-eyed together as we pegged the Starlight Specials through our section. These were special trains hauled by Jubilees, Patriots and Stanier 5's. They ran on a Friday night from London to Glasgow at extraordinarily cheap weekend prices and were made up of the crummiest old rolling stock. They came back Sunday night. There'd be half a dozen, sometimes more. Starlight Specials one after another and people were packed like sardines, standing in the corridors. Our signalbox was on a bend, all trains had to go fairly slowly round and I had a spotlight I could concentrate on the carriages. You'd see them standing — poor people from London to Glasgow having to stand ten hours in that old draughty rolling stock. I hitchhiked to Glasgow one day to have a look. There were a lot of very different very poor people there.

He'd ask me which "side" I'd be on if there was a war. "Wispers'll stand with the Russians." Him and the railway were the first contact of any depth I had with the old world divisions, the solidarity of the working classes, rich and poor, workers and bosses, and the greatness of the Labour movement. But Wispy was an exception. He was individualist. At sixty he'd become a Roman Catholic convert, from nothing. He was married, and on some afternoons when he had forgotten his pack-up lunch we would see his wife as she came down to the box with his forgotten lunch. And also, he said — everybody else said so too — he'd a woman on the side. "Lovely gal," he told me. "I went to see the Fathers, and I said is it wrong because she's so beautiful and such a lovely young body on her. I love her. I can't see no wrong in it. I still love the missus." Wisp, he accommodated a love of the work, the men, the Church, the Labour, the Union, a wife, an only child, a mistress and there was nothing incongruous. Working alone with a man in a box that grew smaller each time I turned up for the eight hour stint, you learnt a great deal about your partner. You learnt to be tolerant. It's closer than sharing a flat, together between the two of you, you have to hold fort over the main lines, two freight yards, the loco shed, making your mashings and looking across at the red fires from the blast furnaces, lobbing your phlegm out of the sliding windows, stoking up the black grate, polishing the fender, learning how to roll cigarettes. And Wisp was a romantic, nostalgic over the passing of the old working class world. He'd give me little lectures. When you're sixty you want to be able to think back to these days, and say thank God it ain't like this now. He had the pride in the job but he prayed that one day the exploitation and the hardship would end. It doesn't matter, he'd tell me, if the pride and the solidarity go to make way for decent money and conditions. It'll be a sacrifice well made. It'll be up to the likes of you to build a pride in other things, better things.

In my first summer at work I had found where I felt and thought my feet belonged. By the time I was ready to go back to school I knew the reins, and I knew the traffic. Up and down the line they called out, "How's our college lad?" and I liked that. I used to go back after working on the railway with an absolute contempt for everyone else in the school, because they hadn't, or so I thought, the faintest idea of life. That freedom of speech meant a licence for much swearing. That working men are not united; have to be bloody minded; need to break if they are to be men. Mine was quite a big school — 900 pupils — and I don't suppose there'd be more than a dozen boys who had any conception of what work was like for the mass of people. Your father can do it, but you have to do it yourself to understand.

I was working in the box in the summer hols of 1956. President Nasser had nationalised the Suez Canal. I didn't pay very much attention except I thought it was another rather silly pompous British thing. Troops on the dockside at Southampton sang "Wish me luck as you wave me goodbye..." Cheerio... jingo, jingo... bye and bye: and they didn't go anywhere. Anne Shelton and Dorothy Squires and other maudlin balladeers topped the British hit parade, and the burgeoning rock 'n' roll actually took a dip. The boys were eclipsed. The boom in Borstal entries dropped, and the world of the Empire returned. I can remember sitting on my stool in the signalbox, listening on the phone to a portable radio a signalman had down the line, and we were all listening to the news bulletins, and the voice of Sir Anthony Eden. I can remember the feeling that ran down the line as they stood behind Eden, the man who was to show them and the world that the Old Bulldog wasn't dead yet, that Britain was still the grimy statue of Queen Victoria, Empress of India, on the town hall square; that they were at the heart of the greatest Empire of all time. They would airlift, drop the paras — and show the wogs how the lion still roared. Cheeky Nasser, he'll be taught a lesson. To my amazement, they all thought it was terrific we were going in: our lads. There was not one man who at that time spoke against Eden, yet one could feel in the tenor of the comments made, a last stand, a knowledge that the Empire and jingo were about to be proven dead: that pre-war Britain could not return: Eden would fail.

We'd watch from our signalbox window, the American USAF trucks roaring backwards and forwards as they did every day to their British bases across the bridge. And they were coming in their cars, shocking pink and bouncy, tail-finned, for the girls at night. Peep: peep. They weren't going to be mobilised: they weren't coming to the aid of the British and the French Empires in the Suez Canal. We hoped — but in vain. It was disgraceful — the Americans didn't support us. "Our allies," said Wisp, "when it suits them." Phlegm out of the window. And it collapsed. The crisis was over. We had lost: and the new world returned, the boys boomed back into Borstal and up to the top of the hit parade.

57

The men in the signalbox — and all up and down the St Pancras line (because we had the telephone) — were completely deflated. Eden had sold them down the river. We'd been beaten by wogs we'd been assured we would lick before breakfast. It didn't mean much to me, but as an observer in a signalbox watching men in their forties and fifties, the effect it had on them was — astounding. I felt sorry for them, but no sympathy, though I kept my mouth shut. They so deeply believed in British muscle, might and right to put foreigners in their place. It was the only time I ever remember them united: easy come, easy go. Brought a radio — they were as large as attaché cases, portable radios in those days — and the serious particular man, he said "disgusting", and so did Wisp the romantic communist. They had never been united on any industrial issues at work, but on that Suez caper, they were. Teddy boys supported Suez, too.

I think it broke, finally, and irrevocably, an older working class generation's loyalty to Britain, motherland. The dream of an Imperial comeback of the Empire's return, was as much flawed as the socialist's land of milk and honey: the Berlin Wall and tanks in Budapest. The men said, as a National Serviceman said to Richard Hoggart whom he quoted in *The Uses of Literacy*, "Life is a permanent wank inside you." The old feeling of failure, of frustration, returned. What had made it worse was that they had been sold down the river by their own. The Labour Party and the Trade Union movement had lost contact. The people were all for Eden, and the left were against both him and the people. The left had become as much a part of the "them" of complication, officialdom and bureaucracy as the boss and the Tories. As the children who won scholarships didn't seem to be of their people any more. And those who became teenage idols, haven't they been corrupted rotten? As Suez broke loyalty with Mother Britain, so rock 'n' roll between children and parents. The men were bewildered. They'd listen to the news, and we — people like me and Young Porky —

58

would tune in to pop music. Old easy come, easy go used to whistle a catchy tune. The strict signalman, he'd listen intently and pronounce "rubbish". Old Wispy, he'd wink, what's it really mean, eh?

I didn't have to break physically from my parents. I didn't have to leave home, although neither of them would tolerate even listening to one bar of the new music. If father ever found the radio tuned to Luxemburg, he'd snap it off: "turn that hooliganism off. I'll take the valves out and then you won't play it." They were pained I'm sure by a lot of my antics, but I was never threatened with having to leave home, being thrown out of the house. It was my home, as long as I respected them and I was free to do as I chose outside the house. My father, pained, was a free-thinking man. Once I came home so drunk he couldn't fail to notice. I'd been pulled up dancing on the billiard tables and was carried fireman's lift, by the taxi driver, and dumped as a bundle on the doorstep of the address they'd found in my pocket — my father said in the morning, very quietly and simply, don't do that again in this house. Your mother and I have a life together that doesn't include drink. What you do with your life is your free decision, although we would... we have... had hoped we'd brought you up to see right from wrong...

I respected my parents and found my own life, without telling them, out there in the pit of the world, the unknown cities of the night, wanting to feel and experience the abyss. I never thought I'd live very long. None of us did. And I didn't know anyone who was old and alive. And by the time I'd got into living my own life as my own life there came this realisation: a reason why I might not survive beyond twenty-five if the world blows up. That was the difference above all others between us and all previous generations. We knew that mankind now had the power to finish life on earth. Man could do what previously only God could do — blow the planet up: the end of the world.

University College

I was a poor boy, well brought up on solid foundations. Brought up clean and decent, to fear God and respect fellow men but not to have much to do with them. Sufficient unto the day and just a little bit more, on the quiet, for a rainy day. I'm better than *Roget's Thesaurus* on this subject. But my parents did believe their children should do with their talents what they pick and choose according to their lights. I did well in learning talents, but forsook the straight and narrow and went into these by-ways where I met such bushy people. Were we really minions in the thrall of some other planet whose purpose would be revealed one day? Was it a deliberate clever ploy by the establishment to let us feel we were having our way, sort the wheat from the chaff and then return with a puritan backlash? No. Don't be so complicated. Surely we were simply doing just what comes naturally. Having a good time, believing in the brotherhood of man as Wordsworth, Shelley and Lord Byron did when they were young. Sowing wild oats and wanting to do it for ever: thinking we could do it for ever. As soon as I could I chose my own life, quite deliberately, rejecting the grammar school escalator. Running from the meritocracy. Stepping across a class. Making a break from semi-detached decency and convention.

My first idea was to be a priest — that was shocking. Thank God social work hadn't become a career, in those days if you wanted to care and be with the poor and down-and-out people, you became a curate. It was a poor boy's goal as acceptable as wanting to be a footballer or a boxing champ, or a gangster — to be a priest, set you apart. Me and David Giddings from the pre-fabs, we both wanted to be priests. Briefly, in my case.

I'd always had a fascination for great men — like the Pope — and I remember the night Stalin died. I was very

60

small and quite moved. This fascination for charismatic leaders who'd arisen from nothing — not Hitler or Mussolini, never, never, but Eva Peron for a time, and certainly Signor Nenni and Nye Bevan for ever. I once wrote a letter to Chairman Mao expressing admiration and I got a reply back like you get from the Queen only on thinner paper, just as nice but thinner. I was disappointed: the envelope was franked without a pretty Chinese stamp.

I went to University, with reluctance on everyone's part. Leicester University. It proved to be the only year of my life I've ever been really unhappy. Opening the door of the Crush Room at the Students' Union, there were crowds of people milling in animation, talking, smiling and happy: clouds of smoke, music, jeans, and activity: suede jackets and black stockings, and loud accents and lots of laughter. Appalled, I wasn't staying there. I went into Leicester town where they were showing Presley's *Jailhouse Rock*. Went into the cinema on my own, and came out with a girl on my arm. Said goodbye at the bus stop.

There were four beds to my room at the students' hostel. One roommate played tennis, one had a cravat — they were nice enough, meant well, with pale pimply faces and black toe-capped shoes and hair, Brylcreemed flat with a parting. They were obviously painfully poor and meek. The poverty of the middle classes and their nervous inhibitions. The beds were — like a mental hospital. The first night, I came back from Leicester town after eleven but before midnight and I was the only one alive in the whole building. Shocking, when I went into the room there were three sleeping figures. But it was more than this. These students had come to University for the better degree and a better way of life, but they'd no curiosity. Their interest stopped at the syllabus and their social round. Tennis, a drink in the village, and going home one weekend in four. Anything like the lively interest in life I'd found in pubs, caffs and on the railway didn't exist. They'd no style. They weren't very interested in themselves — only the plod to succeed in final examinations that were necessary to succeed in life. Succeed, or not be a failure?

I went away every weekend. Thank goodness Leicester wasn't on the Antarctic; I could go to London weekends. Then I started doing it mid-week. Thumbs-up. Back in time for breakfast in the students' hall. Go to bed, lectures or no lectures. The char, she'd come in — but Mister Gosling what's the matter? It doesn't matter. It doesn't matter. I'm all right now.

I liked the staff and made friends. I liked the library, but I hated the students and there was nothing wrong with them. They were all good chaps and girls and treated me okay. When I wasn't hitching to London I'd go downtown to Leicester, and on the bus, one night, there was this sharp, rather soft-featured boy with a great guitar on his back. We gets talking and he invited me to the pub where they do their practice. One night, some weeks later, I went along. The first time I sat in the public bar downstairs and listened to what the regulars said about the band's practice. I watched the band coming down for their drinks. It was interesting. Never saw the kid.

Second time I went upstairs, taking a pint with me. I stood at the back of this practice room and listened. No one stopped me or said owt. They were a good band, good guitarist, and a very flash drummer. Drank my beer and went out. Said nothing. But the kid, the one who carried his guitar on the bus that night, he was the band's leader and vocalist. He must have seen me.

Third time I went to the pub, I took a pint up to the top room and I introduced myself to the singer with the guitar, and I was in. After that I'd drink there pretty regular Monday nights. I liked going there. It was all right. Made a change. If anything turned out it just turned out.

Over the weeks I became a part of the band's feature. To the band itself I was, and to some extent remained, a stranger. But to the pretty boy, the kid singer, I was "the man", a fan with a brain and London connections. I didn't want to take part in selling them down the river on a Tin Pan Alley showboat. Did they want that? I don't think so — except the pretty boy: he'd got stars in his eyes. I said yes, yes, I will, I will, I can — but I didn't want to know. I was quite happy just carrying the drums to working men's clubs. They went down awful at working men's clubs. The rock-a-billy Tuesday act, and they'd get pretty boy swinging his hips and pouting his lips and twitching his thin legs, very Cliff Richardy. He wanted to be a boy-god and it didn't go down at all: it was embarrassing. The thing that went down best was the solo on drums: the men clapped to that.

The band was to enter the Palais talent competition. The Palais was *the* place, with a resident swing band, and every lunchtime, there was a record rock 'n' roll session. Upstairs, in a heart-shaped bar, you could watch the dancers. Some were very good dancers. In that talent competition, we came second, I think. Maybe we came first — but there was another band that got the whole Palais on their feet, Rog Chapman was the singer, and he sang with a pal Alec, and another pal Bill Prendergast. I forget what they sang, but the style was goofy and the sound was a roar. And I perked up and took an interest in them, too. I'd two bands. The pretty boy didn't like the rough lot. He was better organised, equipped, and smart and ambitious. I preferred Rough Rog Chapman, but he hadn't much time for me, though he was a drinker and on the town. It was a very lively town scene: prostitutes, villains, fights, coffee stalls open to two in the morning, Larry the Lamb and Dago, and a Chinese coffee bar. It was good: the pretty boy never went on the town.

By this time I'd taken a flat in the centre of town, along by the prison. And I knew that I wasn't going back to the University for a second year. I was finding a way out without upsetting anyone too much. I'd wander around for a bit: something would turn up.

I hired the Co-op hall on Belgrave Gate. It's now an Indian cinema, but then it was a hall for hire, and I took Friday nights from the end of August. "Chez-Ray Rock" we called it, and 100 people turned up to the first dance, 200 to the second, and so on. I was business manager, originator, stage manager, publicity, ticket puncher, the whole shoot rolled into one. The caretaker had to be pacified.

"I don't mind you having a good time but drinking, well this just won't do, and there's nobody over eighteen and I found sixteen empty bottles of beer under the seats on the side..."

"Did you? Nice bit of pin money if you take the empties back. I'll lend you my carrier bag!'"

"Don't you be funny with me, because your singer, if you can call him that, is using our microphone — not the nice lad — the other one, you know who I mean. It says in the contract you signed, Mr Gosling, you'd better bring your own microphone, and one of them playing records in the interval I saw sitting on our grand piano. The Women's Labour gave us that grand piano last year, and it cost a lot of money I'll have you know, and what are you going to do about what's going on on the stairway, it's not a knocking shop the Co-op Hall, and it never has been, and it never will be while I'm the caretaker."

And in the background, while the caretaker was telling you off, on the dance floor, there'd be farts and burps from one of Rog Chapman's mates who'd loudly whisper — "tell the snivel nosed bastard if he doesn't shut his cakehole we'll play noughts and crosses on his bleeding face."

"It's all right, they don't mean it," I'd say, inanely smiling and watching my back.

The pretty singer was very cut up. He felt I'd used him, and he was getting nowhere.

"I've been led up the garden path. I'm bringing all this gear down to Chez-Ray Rock, giving my all, performing to an audience of ruffians who don't seem to appreciate fine rock ballads, and you're encouraging them. You run these

64

dances very badly. The programme we work out is all knocked out because on the spur of the moment you fancy some dirty old Ted in a bloody drape suit to have a sing and his voice's like a cheese grater."

"A cheese grater?"

"Yes, and Rog and the Rocking Rs are using our equipment, and whose is the drummer? Are they getting paid? Are you ever going to take me to London? I think you're a con merchant."

"And you'll tell your Dad."

And you shrug your shoulders. Will it be tears before bedtime, when Bill Prendergast comes up, while pretty boy's still pouting and waiting for his answer? Tap, tap, on your shoulder, Bill says: "Hey Chez, can I have my money now, please, I got to go on night shift." It's 9.30 and you'll have to persuade someone to do another act.

Ho ho, tick tock, the truth was I had no money. I was borrowing. After the advertising, which was heavy, we weren't making enough to pay everybody. I was paying the bands, both bands, but why did they have to be paid? Why couldn't we all muck in together? No: they were sure — I must be making a bomb, I must have a bit on the side. I'd been to University, hadn't I?

I took a job in a factory — on a production line, boring holes in rubber–metal bondings. It was a very big engineering place, and I did piecework with overtime. You got very tired and your skin went grey and I couldn't think or read after work. It was down to the boozer, and I fell in with the town boys again, and dancing at the Palais. The lads said why don't you hire the hall again, and do some more Chez-Ray? Some weekends I went away. Not a lot, but I went down to Brighton and by chance, in the 42 club on the front met one of those rock 'n' roll impresarios. He said, it's not too late for you yourself, my boy, you can come down to the Metropole tomorrow, here's my card. It was awful. I couldn't. I didn't. I was certain there had to be something else. The heart-shaped bar at the Palais was false. The music business ripping people off. I'd a friend who was a friend of Russ Conway, the pop pianist, and he said, you want to do those dances again, I'll show you how to make money out of the little gits. They wasn't gits. Drinking on the town, back in Leicester, I wanted to operate, but for real, to practise this rock 'n' roll in some way that wouldn't be a rip off, that would be us kids ourselves in control and not the greasy old agents and poncey new promoters. If only I'd been an Italian, or a little stronger physically, the Mafia might have suited me. I wanted to set something up, run an operation, be busy and make things happen, and of course to be a star — not in the world, but in my world. I knew I could be. You just do.

Snack times

There was quite a following from Chez-Ray Rock days. The pretty boy had left but Rog was about. He was too tall and hard to be taken up in these days of pretty faces but he couldn't half sing — his throat was like a beast rather than a bird: he was and still is very good, and we did dances again, and they were so-so. The band did working men's clubs. If only we'd a place of our own, we said, for teenagers who like our kind of music, but we'd let anybody in. We wouldn't have restrictions. And like the Palais we'd play the latest records, but all the time, we'd control the jukebox, and our bands: it'd be a showcase for them. To run our own show. There was a lot of talent on town. Why couldn't people dance to their own, in our image, rock 'n' roll *à la carte,* by the boys for the boys, and girls?

In the Spanish coffee bar, we talked about all these things, in the pubs and in my flat through the night. I'd a skull we called Oscar. I'd ask Oscar. I'd ask teachers, like Dr Ilya Neustadt who I'd kept friendship with from the University. His house was full of Africans. He was educating them to run their own country, take power from the British. It was very exciting. They said it might be possible. There was a charity called Youth Ventures Limited which was Tommy Steele himself and Lord Pakenham and another socialist, Lord Stonham. They were into keeping kids off the streets, and I met them, and they said if I could form our lads into a committee there could be money, premises, and even band equipment.

One bank holiday we went to Skegness, by the seaside. There was a riot on the way back, and coaches were wrecked and the train stopped and lots of youths locked up in Boston. There was a show trial. Did some go down? A lot of probation, and pictures of the wrecked train in the papers and letters about bringing back National Service and the birch.

When I next met the charity, they were very impressed that some of the wreckers were among my friends, and that an intelligent young person had a real relationship with... "Oh," said a lady from Welwyn Garden City, "these are just the kind of people we want" and yes, although it might present a problem if some of these named train wreckers came on to the committee. What a challenge. The problem would have to be faced. And there would be meetings with the Chief of Police, and money would be found because this youth club/coffee bar was going to happen. And so we formed a committee, and Rog said we could call him chairman, if we wanted, if that's what had to be. We had notepaper printed, and I was secretary. None of us were over twenty-one, so a trust body was set up, of university teachers and some Quaker business men and women who could hold the deeds and sign capital things, and Richard Hoggart was the chairman of that and he was very sympathetic and good.

The day-to-day business we conducted ourselves, and the first business was to make me full-time secretary so we could hurry up getting the building. And the first thing I did was find a piece of cheap land behind the Palais and an architect who so quickly designed a new building which would have been like the first super disco gym in England. But the city council wouldn't give permission. Another authority said something else, and to build a new building anyway would take too long: our gang would be out of their teenage and into marriage — and they said why should they work for something they weren't going to enjoy personally. So we went looking for an old building, we ourselves could convert. And that took a dickens of a time. Our committees: their committees. The city council rented us a large old pub, by the Spanish coffee bar, on the town side of the all night transport caff, just up from the central railway station. We were going to convert it into a coffee bar downstairs and upstairs was going to be a dance floor and gym, and work room and it never got finished. It needed a lot doing to it. The coffee bar downstairs, the charity decided had got to be properly kitted out, so we couldn't convert it ourselves. It had to be professionally done. Formica. Modern seating. I remember, even me could bend the fancy metal chair legs, but everything had to be "with it".

Give people the best and they will appreciate it, was the theory. And with all these gadgets and innovations, the envy of half the commercial cafés in the town, we opened, raw kids in charge. We really were in the youth business, dealing with the accountants and the solicitor and setting on cleaners and form-filling and buying bread and keeping meat — operating in the centre of town, in a big way. My mate, fly Jim, was coffee bar manager, and we were open seven days a week, late morning through to early morning. As late as you wanted it. Or we wanted it. Open to all comers and we had our times. It had a life, no doubt about that: of constant turmoil, noise and warfare, blood and sex. How can you be young without it? And although there had been teen canteens before, we were pioneering with a big flame and a lot of noise and we all wanted publicity, to begin with.

The *Manchester Guardian* said, "A youth club experiment — attracting the rough and roaring," and no-one minded. But when the *Daily Sketch* said similar, with a photograph, there was trouble. Teenagers tell stories. They are artful masters of disguise. When our place was revealed in some stark truth in popular papers, mothers and fathers wagged their fingers and said: "Ho... ho... So this is the place you've been telling me about... Well, well... I see now said the blind man I see..." And they didn't like it. I liked the publicity but I was wrong. I should have avoided it like the plague because its effect was to confuse and make hostile our own people.

Some publicity we couldn't avoid. There was a fight outside a rival coffee bar and a policeman got kicked. Some of our lads were charged, and I went to court and gave the vital evidence that it couldn't have been our lads. They tried to discredit me.

"Would you say it's a terrible thing for policemen to be kicked?"

"Depends," said I, "the police that night had started the... aggravation." It was in all the papers. Youth leader says OK to kick coppers. On town I was a hero. Our Chief Constable, Robert Mark, sends for me. I remember him saying across a big desk "watch it", only in long unsmiling sentences. He'd shut us down if we didn't do this and that. He was hailed as a liberal at that time. He was progressive in meter maids and traffic management.

Some of the first committee members were growing up. Some were leaving, family, forces, taking a regular respectable path, making a success of themselves, leaving this dump with a terrible name. Disowning us. The lords and Tommy Steele outfit who'd put a lot of money in, more than we needed, to buy the flashiest Italian coffee machine and the latest model jukebox they were asking why we were taking such a lot of money and not showing much of a profit. The profit was important. The idea was that the coffee bar profits would pay for other youth activities, rather than having them subsidised by the rate- and tax-payers. It was a canny scheme, no doubt about that. They said to me, you're supposed to be the secretary developing this venture. You've been open so long now, where are the mountaineering trips and good deeds, the sponsored swim and the charity walk and the football team? What have you been doing with your time to develop these rough youths into useful...

Ah, well, I'd cough. I did fancy a motorbike workshop. They sent their field officer to report, and there was laxity and moral turpitude on my part. I was lacking the leadership quality, and why does the place seem so full late at night of anybody, tramps, like a transport café? It was always like sitting on a bomb waiting for it to go off. We were in the thick of things, deep in the sticky end of Leicester life. The local trust, Quakers, Richard Hoggart and Norman Scarfe, they kept faith, but it was getting rough and there was more naughtiness than they knew. Than I dare tell them, for they were good, and naughtiness passes. But the police on the streets, plain clothes police, were poking me in the chest. We're going to get you out of town, boy. And the city council, whose land it was, were quibbling. The pressure was on. The compromises coming. It was agreed we must have regular opening and closing times and a proper membership. We must impose a lower and upper age limit. My heart wasn't in it, and we couldn't enforce it. We'd run too long as a late night, open house caff. It could only be enforced if we shut and re-opened with new management.

It was just before Christmas. One Saturday afternoon, I was on my own when some of the big boys, men, came in legless. I couldn't stop them. They pushed me aside, and gave me a hug when I said the rules have been changed, you're not allowed now, it's kids members only. Some had bottles. They drank and had cheeseburgers and were quiet, for a bit they played cards and then there was a quarrel. They started throwing things through the window, into the street, smashing the room up. An office supplies shop across the street took great delight in poking their head in and saying: "We've phoned for the police and told them you're having a riot." A chair leg had gone through our window into a passing bus window. The traffic had stopped. They went into a side room. Jimmy came in, I said, what am I to do. Lock them in. We'd a key and I turned it. They must have known. The police took a long time coming. When they did, they nabbed the lot, and seemed quite pleased and I was prosecution witness on Monday. The police opposed bail. Someone spat at me from across the dock. I, their friend, had turned agin the lads. I'd called the cops, and someone had locked them in that room. I went back to my office above the coffee bar. Knock, knock, a deputation. "My brother isn't going to get his Christmas pud, at home with the family, is he Goso — and it's your fault." Fist. I'd a black eye for Christmas. We closed the place. I went to London until the New Year, and stayed above a pub in Soho, and I can't remember which one.

All through 1960 I'd been talking about the venture, and raising support, and encouraging others, and attacking the existing youth service from the Boy Scouts to the Duke of Edinburgh. I said, plain and simple, though it cared it didn't connect with young people in the rock age. Tin Pan Alley and the Palais de Danse did connect but they didn't care. The commercial operators conned young people's feeling and aspirations. Somebody had to bridge that gap and both connect and care. We did, I said. We were successful — ran a coffee bar ourselves with no adult help. Real espresso. Genuine Coca Cola. Best hamburgers — the very best meat we got from Kettering. We sold a lot of hamburgers, cheeseburgers too. They were for a long time the best in town, and none of us were over twenty-one, and we were signing the cheques. I praised our ways. And when I described my lot as the rough and ready, the unclubbable and the scrubbers of the town, that was what every audience wanted to hear. That was how we raised the money. I'd written my theory, and practice, into a Young Fabian pamphlet and it was published when we reopened after the Christmas fracas. I got another black eye. Nobody wants to be called a scrubber — and to see that in print in Sunday newspapers. My reign was over.

You let us down, they said. Your words, your writing. All us ordinary people thought you'd do something: you raised us up and then you let us down. You glorified the dirty and the seamy, and we wanted something decent. We have pride and dignity and you dragged it through the mud, painting a seedy picture of tinpot bands and grubby louts and a club no decent person would want to belong to — those were your exact words, I quote: a club no decent person would want to belong to.

I remember coming back one night from Oxford, and it was around four in the morning, and as we came in over the bridge into Central station I could see the lights and the open door. Walking down the street from the station and in through the door, and the jukebox was playing and there were two dancing couples, beautiful and slowly soft, and there was one behind the bar. There had been a good take-in from the till, and the coffee was still good and hot and fresh. There was blood on the floor, and the dirt from a fast night. It had a wonderful used look about it. It was an oasis in a city of the dead. The only place open and exclusive; the sort of place where I could feel proud at being a customer.

Anyway, it finished, between ourselves and the local police, and local adult gangsters and bullies making mayhem, greedy, jealous, interfering, grown up, psychopathic criminals muscling into our already naturally young and messy lives. But how many hot spots ever last more than two years?

I wanted us to run our world, and I couldn't develop it beyond a coffee bar. Two black eyes, and I wasn't in a position to. Once violence gets like that, you have to leave. But there was a tragedy before then, that broke my heart. We didn't trust the charity people: it was the only subject that united us. For the rest, when we had a meeting, and we were the committee in charge, we bickered our prejudice. We griped and grizzled and showed off our greed rather than coming together. Jobs for the boys. Perks for the committee. Larks for everyone. As if centuries of being told what to do, generation after generation, and now we had the freedom and the power and we could use it only to smash our dreams before they got off the ground. I include myself. As if you wanted to get back to that factory and school where you knew where you stood: your place was marked, back to that Palais where participation was a raffle ticket for a pair of nylons. We fought among ourselves. Maybe committees can never work, but I'm not going to believe that. Maybe like old Wisp in the signal box you can't have communality, a socialism in a capitalist, greedy country, but I'm

73

not going to believe that. We've just got to try more experiments, different ways of doing youth ventures. That's the time to do it. I still believe in them.

I was before my time. I wanted what almost happened a few years later. Young people running their own businesses in a cooperative revolutionary way. The Beatles tried with Apple later. As *International Times* was run in hippy days. As the *Time Out* collective: as undergraduates at Oxford and Cambridge have done with this and that for yonks.

But I also wanted youth enterprise to be more working class, more punk, more lower orders in control. Why do smart people have to run things? The old people own the record companies? Why is everything the profit and fun and games of those with capital? I wanted I suppose, but this is looking back, to be some kind of Baden-Powell to rock 'n' roll. As the old scout leader institutionalised camping and the outdoor life, I wanted to seize the music and the feeling of the times to change our world. I wasn't strong or big or clever enough. Even if I had been, how can you lead when you don't really believe in leadership? So it goes. We had nice times. I liked talking and went to pretty interesting places.

Skin trade

When my part in the youth club collapsed, I went back to Northampton, and ate humble pie and took to sackcloth and ashes and lived with my parents, and didn't drink and meet people. Just took a job in a leather factory, up in the morning, sandwiches to work, and home at five. To me great surprise I enjoyed it. I almost stayed. It was a small factory, fifty employees. We took in from India scrubbed skin off a goat or a calf and shaved it, doped, dyed, grained and printed it to produce at the finish a skin of leather. These finished skins went to Oldham or Walsall, Montreal or Rotterdam to be made up into small leather goods: handbags, wallets, and bookbindings. We didn't make anything. We only took this crust of an animal and tanned it, finished it ready for the manufacturer. We were in light leather, vegetable tanning.

They started me on a basic of about £9 in take home pay for a flat five day week, seven-thirty to five-thirty. Sometimes there was this Saturday morning overtime, just as at school sometimes there was Saturday morning detention. It was a family firm, owned and controlled by two brothers. One did the selling and the other was factory manager. "Stick to this!" they said, "and there's a job for life here." I was on a printing machine, pressing a hot plate on to the poorer skins, to imprint a pattern of moroccan — or we had crocodile and pearly and peccary and one with just dots like it was Braille. I did hand graining for the better skins. "See how you fit in," the brothers said, "then we'll see about a rise."

There was a trade union, but it was like looking for the Holy Trinity and only interested in money: not in craft. At a national level it said it did things but on the floor you couldn't find it. To get a rise you saw the brothers, nadgered them and kept your mouth shut. "Don't let on to the other men." I got my rise. I was upped to 4/9½d an hour.

"Get to know leather," they said. "You're a clever lad, and we'll give you a bit of responsibility." That week the packer left. "Look," one of the brothers said, "we're in a tight spot. You won't mind helping out in the packing, will you, now you've had your rise." And I was a packer until I left.

And then it hit me. They, the bosses, I was working for them, doing the bits they wouldn't touch, filling in for their convenience. There were no real chances, even for the foreman and him in the Freemasons and a church warden. The bosses did work, but at the interesting bits, taking off the cream for themselves — not just in the money but in the jobs there were to do.

I was interested in leather. I told them that. I didn't mind doing my bit but I wasn't going to permanently sew the rolls of leather into sacking with a needle and some string. And this was a small factory where dirty jobs could have been shared, things could have worked out, we could have all mucked in. But they got me niggled, I felt they were using me. I got to being slow and late every day and when I left there was no love lost. But I remember joy in that place because it was small and we were turning out leather of good quality, with real skill, competitive and worthwhile. You could see our leather on books bound in red morocco, and think that I had a hand on that.

It's a wonderful thing taking the skin of a dead animal and turning it into this living, breathing leather, and it was dying. It wasn't the animal skins that smelt of death but the floorboards of the factory, the sacking, the relationship between bosses and foremen and men.

While I was in the factory I wrote, little pieces. I didn't go out much. It was a time of nursing my hurt, but the pull of Bohemia gradually drifted me back to London. At Coventry Street there were large, light, bright, late night milk bar type cafés, corner houses where you could stand, parade, chat, loll for the price of a coffee. Maybe two hundred people milling about of all classes and a few

76

tourists. Open and easy and busy people: that world has gone — alas I got by. Who feeds you when you are young? And when you can talk, you can get out of anything. Wit wins in a civilised society and the Coventry Street cafés were as civilised as Noël Coward. I went to Paris, again, and that café, La Coupole. To Brussels — repeating the trips I'd done when I was on college holidays.

I carried on talking. What I'd done in Leicester was an unusual experiment and apparently its history sociologically interesting. After my demise, I was invited to talk even more about it and "young people today". Everyone was interested in working class youth. After the factory it was nice to be out again: to be wanted. Nobody did anything about it when I talked to them. That's what I felt — but I'd be paid a little fee sometimes and always expenses. There were new people to meet and I believed in what we'd done. There should be more of it. There had been a principle behind it.

I went to summer schools. The Labour Party had been in opposition for a long time (1951–64). They were interested in listening to bright ideas. The Fabians invited me to a think-tank in Surrey. Brian Abel-Smith drove me about for a weekend in his hoodless sports car. We drank. I think it was iced wine. The weather was lovely and warm. Somebody told me recently they remember I talked a lot about escalators and how difficult it is to step off them. I can't remember.

The New Left invited me to Wharfedale where I remember John Rex played croquet on the lawn. I thought that was so awful. Socialists playing croquet. I wrote a bit for *Granta* in Cambridge. The National Association of Boys Clubs. London School of Economics. I'd have talked to the Bow Group, to Liberals, Conservatives or Communists but they never invited me. At that time Soho was still ablaze at night with little coffee bars, and the New Left ran one — the Partisan in Carlisle Street. Above it they did their magazine. They were the only people taking the new culture seriously and criticising it with respect. The

77

music press in those days dismissed rock music as a fad or as hooliganism. They saw it as a vandal threat to jazz, and to that Ewan MacColl folk-workers-culture. The editor of *New Left Review* was a very modern man, open-minded, a black man. I was very fond of Stuart Hall.

Colin MacInnes

But the man I looked up to, who was my mentor more than anyone else, was Colin MacInnes, and he introduced me personally, took me by the hand, into the London literary scene. He was a handsome, white-haired, white man: a very tall, upper class, high-civilised bitch and sometimes bully who wore pumps and drank whisky. Music was his hobby. How MacInnes would have hated to have thought his life could be divided into work and hobbies. "What is a hobby? Answer me that? Would Moses have had a hobby? Would Kipling?" A change of voice, "Would Kipling have had a hobby? I ask you a factual question now, junior." I didn't know anything about Kipling. Colin MacInnes was always putting questions, and changing his voice in the middle of the sentence. If you didn't know the answer he'd cut you down cruelly, and you could only recover with wit or deference. He was an opinionated man, and he treated me as a capricious Roman emperor treats a favourite. He had lots of favourites. He had even more opinions, and curiosity was his saving grace.

Colin had written three "London" novels that had been great critical and selling successes. Now he was writing essays, becoming the great explorer of contemporary British life. He was my friend, easy to love, very difficult to please, but impossible to be at ease with as lovers very often are. At times he was the master of manners, the custodian of charm and sensitivity itself, while at other times he was venomous — it was dangerous to be in his company — but I couldn't have had a better teacher. I didn't want another, for a long time. He loved London — *City of Any Man's Dream* was the title of a book of photographs he introduced about his favourite city in the swinging sixties. "Swinging?..." I can hear his voice, and the beginning of another story — "Did I ever tell you..." — or another tirade. He was my magic man.

Colin lent me money, got me into and out of many scrapes. I was but one of his many protegés — he loved taking people up, as he loved sparring with adversaries who were his equal. Moody, petulant, he tested his ideas, every day, on strangers in the street, on the young and his disciples. Disciples — he'd have hated that word. If any one was, though, he was the Baden-Powell to the 1960s — he fought for, led and chronicled, cajoled and disciplined the formation of our compassionate, permissive society (abortive though it may now be in part). The age of affluence, the new working class youth, with money in its pockets, the coming of drugs, multi-racial Britain, Colin welcomed, put in perspective, championed and could correct. He was the great scout-master to the new-lifemanship and gamesmanship, and the changing English tongue. Unfortunately, or fortunately, the 1960s were not to be an age for Baden-Powells. Our new liberated times were to be ruleless, and a denial of roots for us John Bulls, jumbos, white Englishmen certainly. Colin was half-British, a descendant of Kipling but he loved the times: he subscribed to the philosophy of anti-leader. He never became a cult figure, he never wrote his *Scouting for Bisexuals*. Lesser men, experts and maharishis, took the later limelight and the potential of Colin MacInnes was never fulfilled. I couldn't bear to see him, bitterly grumpy in his later years, after the 1970s had soured the easy pleasure and the promise of the sixties.

He was a very physical man, with great presence, and the style of his day-to-day, night-to-night living was as important as his published words. He should have had a Boswell, but his temperament could never tolerate anyone for very long. Or vice versa. He was the tall cat who dances on his own. He had by choice no home, no family, no known children. He was dedicated to living the literary life, and being free. Never a bank account. Cash in folding money, walking money, as the Irish call it.

He was lodging near the Oasis swimming pool, at the top of Shaftesbury Avenue, when I was his guest in a flat he'd cuckooed. This was 1962–1964. I'd ring the bell, and stand on the pavement. Eventually a window would open. He'd look at me, close the window and there'd be another long wait. Keys would then be thrown down, wrapped in a knotted handkerchief. "Catch." I'd let myself in and he'd be there, smoking, with a smile, a thought and a bottle of whisky. Even if he'd had to borrow the money, there would be the whisky. Colin couldn't live without being generous.

"There is a glass, junior, make yourself welcome. Should the phone ring do not answer. Modern conveniences, are they not for us to use as we fancy? We are not their slaves. If you write a letter, and mark upon the envelope Urgent, to whom is it urgent? — the sender or receiver? Please state: be precise. See you in a little while."

For Colin I'd have to wait maybe an hour or two, sometimes longer, while he retired to a back room, a simple single bed, table and clattering typewriter. Few papers or books but kept meticulously tidy.

Eventually he would emerge, white, close-cropped hair, a John Wayne of a man with beautiful skin, in a white T-shirt and blue slacks like a football coach, with white socks and fine Italian shoes one day, pumps the next. "Always wear one article of class about you, or conversely, one article of casualness." He dressed with the same exactitude with which he used our common language.

He'd lecture, hector, play games with me. He enjoyed with relish goading my provinciality. He loathed provinciality. I could be small minded and Colin was a world citizen. He'd constantly upbraid the English with their imperial guilt: the white Anglo-Saxon Protestant. "Cromwell: you'd have liked Cromwell? And Harold Wilson: who is his Milton?" I was good game. As swift as I could be. He didn't always catch me.

He was a colonial, Australian Scot. I remember with what glee he threw at me John Prebble's *Culloden*. Colin was helping to give the British Empire back to the natives with grace, and make them proud of their own history. I remember his pressing upon me a bundle of reprints of an article pleading for the return of the Elgin marbles from the British Museum to Greece. "Distribute these to your provincial intelligentsia..."

"Follow me" — and I'd do that every time. On to the street. "Taxi —" To a gallery for Sidney Nolan; to a lunch he'd organised to honour Robert Graves; to Beatrix Miller with his script when she was editrix of *Queen* magazine; to pay respects on Colin Ward, the editor of *Anarchy;* to a party at Mark Boxer's: Colin loved parties and being alternatively the charmer and irritant. Walking Soho. Stopping George Melly on his motor scooter for a "Good day" and an argument. His club was Muriel's, the afternoon drinking club on Dean Street where Colin would shine above the competition: sparring with Paul Potts (verbally), with Frank Norman (almost physically). Frank Norman was the darling of the time because he'd been in nick: a villain who'd taken to writing, thoroughly enjoying being lionised by the establishment. There was Francis Bacon. A taxi to the Mangrove in Notting Dale: Dale not Notting Hill. Up and down the town. East: west. A man not famous but with a reputation. Two knocks on a door and a club would open. To a Greek restaurant where he'd pursue, to the amazement of the management and waiters, his arguments for the return of those Elgin marbles. It was embarrassing to be with him, and such fun, as with deft word play he'd get himself out of the scrape he'd got himself into.

MPs? — he had no time for power. Fabians: the same. At the end of the Second World War, Colin had found himself in charge, momentarily, of a camp for civilian German prisoners. Colin let them out: all of them.

Every moment of his life he made memorable. We took a minicab one night. Minicabs were the latest London craze. We went into Broadcasting House — there were no passes in those days. Colin found an empty recording studio in the basement and played me Billie Holliday like disc jockeys never do — listen to the words — play it again — that phrase — listen to the meaning — that is only one meaning — now listen to that phrase again and tell me another. Testing you all the time, and himself against you.

He was a teacher, a preacher, a writer who'd loved to have been a song-and-dance man — but he wasn't. And his writing was of essays rather than drama documentaries for the television. A pity maybe, for he had the keenest eyes of his age for social observation. He could spot trends before anyone else, and make judgements upon them. He wasn't frightened of taking moral positions. He had this sense of history, and put fashions of the moment into perspective, and enjoyed making prophetic guesses, many of which have come true. But it was all at a high Bohemian table, in the great literary tradition.

He was so proud I remember that it was an issue of the *Spectator* rather than the *New Statesman* that printed his thoughts on crime and punishment. Proud it was the *Spectator,* a radical conservative paper — you can be radical and a conservative. The left are as full of bullies... would you have been a Cavalier or a Roundhead?... Our species, we may divide, may we not, into Greeks, Romans and Jews... Harold Wilson is a Jew?... Winston Churchill was a Roman with a dash of Greek in his temperament?...

Sometimes in the early sixties half the weekly magazines would have pieces in by Colin, or letters about previous MacInnes articles. He was the essayist of the period, but not in magazines like *Melody Maker*. He was not a brain on the *Brains Trust,* nor a television guru — though he tried. He was great for trying. I remember an interview he did on a television programme with Brendan Behan. It was embarrassing because Colin was so fulsome in his praise. He couldn't be a bitchy critic: a satirist. Public confrontation was not his style. He was a promoter: dealing with subjects he held in critical esteem and righteous enthusiasm. He would watch the gurus of the day, Malcolm Muggeridge and young David Frost, hating their standards and jealous of their influence. He was terribly hurt his three London novels were not made into films — *A Clockwork Orange* by Anthony Burgess was, with its violence and fantasy, make believe sex, drugs and rock 'n' roll, but not Colin's straight, wide-eyed look at social phenomenon and reality with modest affection. From a colonial distance he observed the changes in English society with faith, morality and optimism — and never got filmed. They never filmed *Mr Love and Justice* about the humanity in both copper and ponce, *City of Spades* about the new black Britons, and *Absolute Beginners* about the first teenagers. I was around Colin when film producers were sniffing, but the films never appeared.

It was to Tim Raison's newly founded *New Society* magazine that Colin turned to write a weekly column of social observation. Here were his best essays. Before the sinecured professional sociologists monopolised the market with their cleverness and unspoken vested interests; before the grubby compromises of Labour Government. Colin wrote, free from cant, free from party — independent, outspoken and rational. In a way, looking back, I suppose we can think of Colin MacInnes as the last great independent literary essayist and man of letters in the tradition of Dr Johnson and George Orwell. He had an almost eremetical devotion to his craft and was forever extending his interest, into gardens or Gilbert and Sullivan. Yet his best pieces were based on today's life. He believed in the young. "Don't pay me back," he would say when he lent me money, "unless you become rich, and then remember when you are older do the same for your youngers." He was no beat or hippy to look at; he practised what he believed.

He was a considerable letter writer and one of his last letters was to *Gay Left,* congratulating gays for at last

84

(1976) producing a thoughtful magazine, and saying simply, like the wise old man to our generation he'd become: please remember the fight for sexual liberation will probably have to be fought all over again in each generation. He was a considerable befriender. He was Michael X's pal. Held the hand of Richard Neville at the *Oz* trial (metaphorically). A modest guru: a real teacher in an age that has since become overfilled with noise.

He was a real fighter for liberation in those early battles of the sixties that fired us. He sought out freedom lovers and gave them comfort. He appreciated the villain in every copper, the golden heart in every whore: the paradoxes of life. A brave, wily, wary-less man, he walked proudly in where others would only dare to peep. He hunted in the then uncharted corners of our new society. "How," he said to me in a Chinese restaurant, "do I get inside the Chinese community. They are the most difficult." He hated defeat. He had to believe all permutations were possible. "Read all the classics you can before you're twenty-five," he said. "Read, read and learn — then you can live and act." Our generation didn't do that. We thought the time for reading would come later. Maybe the next generation will learn from our mistakes — and among the classics they should read Colin MacInnes.

But slowly I did begin to earn more from my writing some weeks than I would have got in the leather factory. I now had a network of friends; Joan Elliott in Newcastle, Charles Parker at Birmingham's BBC radio put me in his folk documentary on youth revolt and I stayed, just hanging around while he put together a documentary on lorry driving through the night and people struggling against poliomyelitis in the iron lung. I'd places to stay all over Britain — I loved touring — Trevor Griffiths, Alan Rooney, Albert Hunt. Manchester, Edinburgh, Leeds. It could have been anywhere the wheels stopped for no particular reason. Plymouth, Bradford, Cardiff — any town of that sort of size, with a town society it's easy to fall into and be somebody, do something. Writing wasn't enough. I wanted to do something again — or be in a position to.

A room in another town

I came to settle in Nottingham on the rebound, still on the rebound from that youth club; having to look behind, over my shoulder all the time for the debts and threats and general odium seemed to follow me everywhere. I don't mean official things. I've never fiddled in my life, in any public things I've had. I mean this — that the young get attached. I'd had a full life with one full life. I'd run away. Now I wanted to settle and wherever I ran I bumped into chums from the youth club days. "Hey up, Chez, black eye gone, my old mate, how's tricks... You was one of the lads weren't you?... Did you really lock that door, you know?... What you mean you can't remember?... Let's have a drink eh, and forget about it... Do you remember?... Bloody times we had, eh — have another..."

When I came to Nottingham I was twenty-four. I had ideas of writing a book about England. Richard Hoggart said I should. To follow Daniel Defoe and J.B. Priestley on a journey and show the strengths in our people — so many good people and such a down-in-the-dumps country. And in all its differences — regionalism was just coming into fashion. I'd accumulated a lot of material.

When I came to Nottingham my entrance was dirty, anonymous and at night. I wanted to know no-one to begin with, apart from noddies. Nod to people in the street and get a wink back. Nights on this town. Nothing but Christian names, and only again by chance. No address swapping. No calling. No promising. Let chance turn the wheel. I took a room but I was always going away. When I came back it was frequently dirty, defeated and loaded in clouds of steam and grit in the eye, on trains that swayed like something out of Emile Zola. There were few passengers conveyed at night. The trains ran because they'd always ran and I boarded three sheets to the wind. On strange cross-country routes, I laid myself out on the last wooden, slat-seated expresses, a smooth amber wood. They'd have come from Oxford, Marylebone, York, Manchester. I'd sleep — fitfully enough to often miss getting out at the station, and be carried forward through the canyons of this town to be roughly woken miles further north or south or east or west. The porter calls the police. There are stubborn questions. Laconic answers. What else can they do? Waiting in waiting rooms. Coke up the nose. Dozing on elbows. Lying on tables as if L.S. Lowry would arrive to paint one's portrait. A sallow-cheeked freak, red eyed until another draughty rattling train would take me back. Steam trains romantic? Tell that to the handkerchiefs. In the dawn and stopping train, hooting through the choking soot and fog of coalmine counties, the ash fields and the pit humps. Arguing again with the guard. Refusing to pay the excess. "I'm making an involuntary journey."

"All you have me old sunshine is a platform ticket. Name? Address?" Seven Stratford Square, Shakespeare Street, was a cold water pad, a little room, barely furnished, bare boards and rough boards. The sheets as thick as a split sheet of a Kleenex paper handkerchief. Cold water tap, and the concierge below — Ma Marriott banging with her poker on the ceiling.

"I know you got somebody in that room. I can hear you. I can have you out in the morning. I'll see Mr Carter. You mark my words."

Never let her in. Never tell and pretend in the morning it hasn't happened. Her legs were bad, she'd never get up, swollen with gin, sitting over a coke stove. She was a lady of that certain shape now gone out of fashion, almost completely out of existence — a baggage.

The agent, Mr Carter in the agent's office, he liked me. My excuses amused him. I was young looking and versed (London trained) in the arts of charming people off perches, and quite hardhearted. If the victim wasn't deaf

and couldn't fly, or fell on to the banana skin of my
stories, and I heard about the nettlebed of trouble I'd got
the helpful soul in, then that just made a more colourful
day: another moment.

"Pay the rent next week, Mr Carter — that okay? —
and something off arrears week after."

I think when I left there it was less than a pound a
week. When I began it was twelve-and-six. It wasn't
much but it was a key, a bed, and it didn't leak.

"Promise Mr Carter: when I get this cheque tomorrow..." Smile. No social security. Never had the social.
Smile at Mrs Marriott: spend on buying her a box of
chocolates before the rent.

"A little drink Mrs Marriott?" in the afternoon. "I seen
Mr Carter." Chocolates and gin before the rent. Flaunt
and dare. It was easy to get by, if you gave it your
attention: with charm and wit and the lust of a country
boy for life in another town with no parents to be seen
fretting; no friends and relations to bump into; no school
acquaintances to cross my path and say: "What line have
you finished up in Gosling — married yet?" I don't want
to hear those questions. There is no life but what you
make it. People must do that today.

A generation has passed while I've been in this town.
I slipped in and stayed for fifteen years. The
Nottingham Victoria railway station I arrived at has
gone, been pulled down and in its place they've built a
multi-million pound, multi-level indoor shopping centre
everybody said could never succeed. It has. Old Ma
Marriott's, where I had my first bare room in 1964, it's
now a ginormous polytechnic students' college. Everyone said they'd never find enough students. They have.
I still live in Nottingham, but I don't "live" any more. I
have a house. I have a private life. I belong to a club —
another club I helped to build but I don't go very much.
I don't go to any club. I have a library ticket — that's all
that's in my pocket, no credit card. I'm getting less and
less into possessions.

Once I was a member of every club, a man of town, on the town — in my provincial way — a man of fashion I became and of vigour and I cut a figure and built an empire in Nottingham. Today I sit on a few committees that do good works, reluctantly as few as I can get away with out of loyalty. I don't want to take part. I don't want to live here any more. Not life with a capital "L". I've retired from the streets. I walked. I did. Not today thank you very much. I'm older than Jesus now. Half way home. I'll soon be older than George Orwell or D.H. Lawrence when they died and I have to ask myself what have I done? Ask, before it's too late to do anything about the answers.

I had thought I'd be dead at twenty-four, like James Dean, immortal: to die with the bloom of promise still on your cheeks. The young vanish. I nearly died in those final fracas days of that teen canteen, and then when I came to this town life began again. It was Nottingham, but it could have been anywhere.

It's Saturday

I came to this town to escape. A head in need of a bed
before the word hippy was used on the streets. Alongside
The White Negro by Norman Mailer, the pamphlet that
defined the hipster, I could set my own little Fabian
pamphlet *(Lady Albemarle's Boys)* on the organisation of
youth clubs. The *New Statesman* was bought for pieces
about beatniks as a way of life in Brighton by Royston
Ellis or was it Roy Kerridge? I wrote book reviews for
Tribune, a column for *Peace News* and my first glossy
piece about a place called Ironbridge for *Town* magazine
just after it had changed from *Man About Town* to simply
Town. Michael Heseltine owned it and Nick Tomalin was
the editor. Nick had developed a theory of "conspicuous
thrift": haute couture fashion was going down a class, the
with-it upper class young were to wear Levi jeans and
drive Mini Cooper cars and live in Habitat bare-furnished
flats in Rotherhithe and eat bangers and mash. That was
to be with it. He could write, Nick Tomalin. I couldn't do
so well. He had to lock me up in a room to get the piece
on Ironbridge finished. I wasn't a very easy writer, nor
very fast. I carried on. Went away and came back. People
came to see me, now I had a little room. Philip Callow.
Paul Potts was my friend. Jeff Nuttall produced his *My
Own Mag.* Colin MacInnes continued to write me letters
that began "Dear Junior..."

Oh, there were lots of nice people and contemporaries:
Ken Howard, Alan Blaikley, Paul Overy doing little
pamphlets — *Axle Spokes* — for ordinary newsagents to
sell, explaining the new renaissance. There was Cordley
Coit, an American photographer who lived in Paris and
had been taking photographs of Ornette Coleman, the
jazz musician, when I met him. His wife was educated at
university here and she'd bought a caravan to live in by
some gravel pits on the edge of town. She'd left college

91

some years previous, and was now busy in London and New York. She'd told Cordley to come over and wind up the caravan. He stayed a few days and he drank on the town and taught me to cook chili con carne. When he went away he took me back with him to Paris where he'd a flat by the Sèvres Babylone metro station. Paris again but this time with the key to a flat. I stayed some time. And more than once. On the metro one night I was reading the next day's *Herald Tribune* and wondering how I could write for that. Glancing down the small advertisements for eating out at all the smart places in Europe, from Berlin to the Algarve, from Iceland to the Mediterranean, there was only one entry for England outside London — the Kingfisher, Mansfield Road, Nottingham, for premier fish and chips, eat in or take out. I was proud.

Provinciality was proud then. Now it's just accepted. But then the old order and a new dawn co-existed. New cocks of the north were panting for room at the top, but the old geezers were still in charge ruminating in their sunset days of British brass, watch-chain and waistcoat. Our town had a stock exchange of its little own. There were gentlemen's clubs with smoking and billiard rooms called the Reform and the Constitutional. I never went but I knew where they were. You saw the waistcoat and the watch-chain men through glass windows. Sometimes they sat in the street on their shooting sticks, in their tweeds and caps. The gentry were in observable fixed positions. The middle class took tea. Their chinless children went to the coffee bars. Saturday was *the* day, in the morning, in the Kardomah coffee shop on Market Street. All the sets met. People began gathering about eleven and the attraction of this coffee shop was its having two rooms. On the ground floor, middle class ladies sat, melting their gateaux, munching the nut fillings and sipping their coffee. We had to walk through their tables to reach the back stairs and walk up to the room where the young sets met. Having to walk through a garden party of ladies did need a certain courage. It kept some riff raff out.

The Kardomah was a daytime coffee shop and upstairs where we met was the place. You could sit at a table by the window and watch the passing street. There was no muzak but the buzz of conversation. We read newspapers and often ordered nothing: "Just waiting for a friend," you'd say to the nippie. That was quite acceptable. Peter Price sometimes came. He was CND. Buy me a lemon tea, if I asked: "Got no money, Peter." They did nice lemon teas, in a glass held by a metal frame with a long silver spoon. If no friends arrived, you'd leave, easily and hassle free as we say today. Waltzing through the ladies' tables downstairs.

It was a mixture of middle class young people and Bohemians of all classes, and a much more leisurely clerk class that seems to have disappeared — like assistant bank managers. Banks and most offices were open on Saturday mornings, at this time, and few places had their own canteen or staff club. I do believe that the staff/works club/canteen has ruined our town life as much as or more than the motor car.

That Kardomah has shut. It's been closed some years. It'll never re-open. That way of life has gone. The office workers who took their breakfast there while I was still in bed still do that today, but in a staff facility. In those days they took their breakfast and their coffee break, their lunch and cup of tea in public places. They were the bread and butter of the coffee shop trade, that enabled our mid-morning crowd to lead our free and fancy life.

Saturday mornings were where introductions were made, people pointed at down there on the street. Whispers in the ear of who to avoid. The chocolate gateau was delicious, and they did toasted cheese sandwiches. Toasted sandwiches were the newest thing. Didn't the toast have its crust removed? Dainty for ladies; freaky for us. There was a man whose name I never knew who was forever about to start a local literary magazine. There was Dave Turner who sang skiffle folk music in pubs at night. There was a very posh, tall, coffee-skinned youth I called "the last of the mulattos". I loved words like that. He was seven foot tall with a double barrelled name. Later he went into textiles, made some money, joined the Labour Party, and entered Parliament. There was another black boy who was even blacker. He was very black, very handsome, very charming and a hustler with it. Miney loved him. We all loved him. He lived off us all. He never had to ask. And if you were in his company, you got fed too.

There was always gateaux for Courtenay: dinner parties, daughters and rides in motor cars. He was ace for two seasons: the black beauty in the Kardomah coffee shop upstairs — Courtenay Tulloch — he had this Scots name. I said, one day you'll be head of the clan. If I close my eyes I can hear you laughing, with the world at your feet. He came to Manchester with Miney and me for the telly, and then to London. He became black correspondent for the early *International Times*. Edited his own paper in Westbourne Grove, he called it the *Hustler*. Courtenay was a lieutenant at the Black House of Michael X in Islington. That was a remarkable scheme. In the early sixties, the idea was to have in one place a proud display and workshop, restaurant and dance and all black art. Whatever became of that? Michael X left and then got hanged for murder in the West Indies. The Queen wouldn't give him a reprieve. You, Courtenay, are you still a prince of Black Power? Where are you? Do those white coffee bar days mean anything to you? Did they wind you up, give you the courage to walk out — as they did to me.

Wouldn't you remember H.H.? He was older than us, dimmer and not as smart. He'd been famous since Forest won the Cup in 1959. H.H. had been having a party, Burns Street way, when the police came to cease the noise, and, as the coppers were banging on the front door, H.H. tipped the contents of his piss pot on the silly coppers' nuts singing, "We won, we won the Cup." When there was only one cup to win. There was a terrible racket. It was in the papers, and then rumoured that H.H. was planting marihuana seeds in corporation roundabouts, the pride of the Parks Department. Ever since H.H. lived off his legend. His livelihood for a decade was assured. "Marihuana mmmnn!": the graffiti is still there. It is not entirely scrubbed away, you can just see it in the brickwork. "Babies are dying in Biafra" was overprinted, finally, in 1978 by the Anti Nazi League, but "Marihuana mmmnn!" you can just make out, like a ghost on the recreation ground wall. They said H.H. wrote it. Was he a dealer? I felt honoured and warm in his company, though he was a most uncommunicative soul: a thin, still, silent, solitary man, a scruffy white man of skiffling days. "I'm worried now but I won't be worried long." Washboard and tea-chests. You talked to him, but he didn't talk back. If I passed him today on the street would I recognise him? No. Were the stories true? It didn't matter. He was a Kardomah coffee bar legend of his time, a man fabled in the gossip of the summer straws, an inspiration to the young. He had only to walk the streets and he was Godot. Live for the moment. To be outrageous. "It is forbidden to forbid." I did a lot of pub crawling on my own for preference, picking up and dropping in on the way. To the Hole in the Wall for rock 'n' roll. One of the few pubs with a jukebox licence. They were hard to find. To the Bell, randy with students and New Orleans jazz, live and no admission. To the Albert for a big barmaid, Veronica, with arms like tree trunks and a voice like the wrath of God. To Yates for the violins. To the Towers for whores and blacks. The Towers has gone. The Albert too. The Bell hasn't changed, still owned and run by one man and his mum, one family, a free house. Most places have changed utterly.

We'd cross town to the George, a coaching inn — still there but not the same. In those days it had a snooty little back bar called the Dickens where posh camp gays met as a freemasonry. They all knew one another. They were a club — only anyone who dared could walk in. They wore gold rings on fifth fingers and were the most frightful snobs. There was the Queen Elizabeth for fights, every night. They all closed at ten. And when the pubs shut, a lot of time was spent walking the streets. There was a choice of night coffee bars — this one rough, that one students, that one pretty gay. There were three next door to each other opposite the mining and technical college: El Sombrero, the Fifty-Nine, and another with a Spanish sounding name. Then the authorities relaxed the licensing hours, legalised homosexuality, permitted gaming machines and these little palaces of pleasure, these little corners of canoodling and conversation, are today all car parks. The gays came out of their closets and set up discos of their own. The gamblers went into their closets. Bookies were on the streets when I began. Now we have betting shops.

What a fuss I'm making about coffee bars. What was there ever there but hot dog and cream cake late at night? More food than a nightclub. But it was very nice: our gamey life. You could have egg on cheeseburger. There were recesses where lovers could snuggle for the price of a cup of espresso coffee. Sometimes, somebody, anybody would pick at a skiffling guitar, unamplified. These places cost nothing to enter. Nothing but an espresso to stay a long time. Pick somebody up, easily, frequently; late at night there were always mysteries without a bed. Sometimes you remember an earlier invitation to a party, and the coffee bar was a pause before drinking recommenced in those clubs that had bedrooms: that's a party.

Home with the milk. Milk: I was never sufficiently stable to order milkman-delivered milk. Now I do, and I haven't been to a party like that for years. With all our change, with all our advancement, with all our reforms, and affluence and humanitarian measures, with all our liberated leisure provision, have the legally licensed clubs of today the atmosphere of those old coffee bars? Do liaisons happen like they did, can anybody enter for free? Is there the breadth of humanity?

All across town there was only one nightclub, and you had to queue to get in and they didn't always serve alcoholic liquor. It seemed to depend. It was a little place, tiny with low beams, in the Lacemarket district, above a pie shop, up some narrow stairs. You needed an introduction, or to be a known and fancied/wanted face. You had to queue in the street, and when you got to the door you had to charm or card your way in past the genial Albert and his pal. Albert was a marvellous, fat and jovial, right wing, working class Tory, a poor white's rights champion from a slum district he later represented on the city council. Albert had a passion for jazz, and his part interest in the one nightclub in town.

The poet and painter Adrian Henri came to see me. His sister, Avril, became a lodger in my flat. Adrian would stand on the road, tickled pink by green buses that went to a suburb called "Arnold". Fancy a bus called Arnold, said Adrian: "A sixty-nine to Arnold." We'd giggle and tickle ourselves like silly schoolgirls, standing on the pavement, bemused as Laurel and Hardy at the sight of yet another bus called Arnold. "Come in Arnold your time is up." Just Arnold: so silly.

At night the delight was this nightclub — Adrian christened it the pea curry club. They had real nightclubs in Liverpool that sold booze through heavy metal grills. But in my sodden town, so much more provincial, there was only this. But they didn't do pea curry in Liverpool, so booze or not we could tickle each other and keep going back with laughter to the bar asking for yet another bowl of pea curry, please. The curry was spooned from a huge tureen into the tiniest of china hand bowls, with a plastic spoon and "D'you want mint sauce?" Grown in Albert White's back garden? It was more a sample than a meal.

The club seemed to have an occasional haphazard licence. Sometimes, and sometimes in the presence of policemen, doors would be locked and the queue turned away. Bottles of beer would appear from beneath the bench seats, crates of light ale from behind curtains and wasn't whisky sold over the bar behind the pea curry, in plastic beakers? They were the first plastic cups I ever remember, in the pea curry club. And the fellow next to you would take a saxophone from a box and blow right beside you, musicians would jam all over the place, live jam until two, three or four o'clock in the morning. When it happened oh oiks, what larks, what lollypops there were in my green apple days in this town.

CND on Sundays

I liked Sundays. Hanging about the Square. Cartoons at the Scala. Was the Robin Hood café open Sundays? I think it was. Marjorie's Guildhall Tavern was shut, and the Robin Hood was open in the afternoons. That was nice. Down a few steps, a window view of passing people's feet and legs. You never saw the faces. Had to guess? And on one of the walls of the café were masses of signed photos of stars, held beneath big sheets of plate glass so they wouldn't get greasy. Real stars of variety — on Sundays they'd rehearse, slipping across to the café in their slippers for a jug of tea to take across. Lorry drivers — you don't see those in town any more. Young rock 'n' rollers, and a better class of tramp than you seem to get today. More roadster than derelict. I took a tramp home with me one night. Didn't we all. He was very nice. A bit articulate, but he ate the food and grunted he'd welcome a bath. He fell asleep in the bath and then he peed the bed. He had nice table manners. I think these tramps were given a meal ticket by some society that they could exchange at the café for a square meal. The food was very good. Best eggs, chips, with all the trimmings. My friend Brin still talks of the best cold chicken salad: chicken breast and as much salad cream as you wanted. Cold Coca Cola was cold and a banana milkshake to follow: big, with a long spoon and a whole banana slit longways. We'd have two sometimes.

I liked Sundays. The band played in the park. I liked Lyon's tea shop on my own. There isn't anywhere you can get a cup of tea now. Lyons was a real tea shop — lovely tea with a currant bun, and people moving around the table. Maunge about and smoke a little. Cartoons at the News House, playing musical chairs. Sally Bash outside. They rattled their tambourines down to the square where they held a service, wet or fine, they marched away behind their flag and were religiously followed by the Communist Party who brought a soap box, the real thing, pulpit-like, along with them in a little van. The Ethical Society, they came too. Individual Pentecostals. I always admired one regular who served bacon in a very good grocers. You could set your clock by the Communist Party. Their platforms had ledges for notes and a drawer for pamphlets. I came to admire the man who did their Sunday soaps, Mr Peck. He'd leather patches on his sleeve elbows, a tweedy jacket, grey flannels and a cardigan. The British Legion badge in his buttonhole. Poppies every November, "Lest we forget". He was so proud he had fought fascism and had been in the RAF when we and Russia were allies together. Now he loyally stood by the old alliance, in spite of the uprisings in Hungary and Poland and Czechoslovakia later. Not without feeling. Not without pain — but he stood by his Russian comrades and never left the Party. At the end of every argument, fascism was vermin, capitalism for the few and in spite of all its faults Russia is the worker's friend. Comrades... "The Tories who tried to scrap our civic theatre are the direct political descendants of those who opposed the opening of the first public library in 1868, brothers and sisters, on the ground that reading would be dangerous to the contentment of the workers."

The square on a Sunday was like watching a trooping of the colour. There was a real ritual to it and big audiences. Speakers all speaking at once like a bank of television sets tuned to different stations in a shop window and they spoke sincerely and made sense. I really liked old Tom from the Ethical Society, he was like the son of Tom Paine. He never went for a drink afterwards. The Christians didn't either. CND did. They were slap happy about speaking, and sometimes only turned up to drink afterwards.

CND also held public meetings in the week, at the Friends' Meeting House, a modern building in the Swedish style of light and wood. I sometimes went to hear

100

the reasoned arguments, in reasoned tones by reasonable respectably dressed people, that Britain should stop making the atom bomb, and take her own initiative, unilaterally disarm and set a moral example to the world. It was all sensible. I agreed. What could we do? During question time, people I'd seen on the square soapboxing would try to break the Quakers' peace and style. They'd swear and shake their fist but you never got a Quaker to lose his temper. Some of the Sunday raughters had discovered there was a regional seat of government where the top politicians of the town would go for shelter and to be safe during a nuclear war. They were for physically occupying these loony centres. But direct action the Quaker way would always be peaceful. And after every meeting they smiled on everyone and proffered coffee in small, thick cups.

There was a mass meeting — billboards, leaflets, advertising on the buses too, and a rally in the Co-op hall for which a very large audience turned up. "Faces" from the television were there and there was much apologising for the absence of — was it Elizabeth Taylor and Richard Burton or Stanley Baker who'd sent a telegram? Afterwards, the CND campaigning leaders retired for a sherry and those sandwiches with the crusts removed in a private room at the coaching inn, the George. I didn't understand these up-town dos. Why didn't they have them with the people, in the upper room of big working class boozers with pork pie and pints of bitter beer? There was a similar sip-and-crustless occasion for the Kenyan Independence Day celebrations. Paid for by the Kenyan government as a tribute to the local branch of the Movement for Colonial Freedom. They seemed to have so much money to throw around, I thought of asking them to pay my electric bill. Being cut off at that time. After the sherry at the CND rally, the two professional CNDers — George Clark and my pal Stuart Hall — were captured from the Quakers, and taken to a Bohemian house for real beer and political guts with the Sunday speakers

101

from the square. That house I remember as a place of constant heated political argument, that night for the rage, drunkenness and chaos and the way the two national campaigners, tired out, hung on to their dignity.

Opening time on Sundays was seven, and the CND roughs and the CP zealots would tail away to the Flying Horse hotel. It was a hotel then with a real restaurant that smelt of broth and buttered leeks and fresh fruit. Today it's not even business men's deals — nothing but burnt flesh and disco. It was a hotel. Now it is a steak bar with duckling and rooms. Oh it was so lovely: the real county town hotel the townspeople could use. There was a long room, oak panelled, where you could only be served by a waiter, and here on Sunday night the political agitators went and sat at tables on chairs with arms 100 years old, dusted and never having to be restained.

There were loose Indian carpets on a wooden floor, and that sound that has now gone from public houses — the buzz of conversation. Outside, rent boys stood, and shy boys from the country too frightened to enter alone this mahogany-looking hotel, supposedly full of businessmen and in fact full of businessmen, communists, whores and queers. "Would you like a good time dear?" In those days there were sexual transactions more open and available than in today's so-called permissive society. Flaunting the illegal. The girls risking a £2 fine for soliciting. The men risked more — but did it on the street. I don't know? Maybe nobody saw it altogether except me. Maybe the communists didn't notice the boys. Maybe the businessmen turning their buttered leeks didn't notice the communists. It's all gone — for duckling and disco.

The Communist Party had a physical HQ downtown. They don't today. The National Front do, but the Communist Party don't. Then they did: above a restaurant in a district where they had assize processions, walking through these gloomy narrow streets, alley-wide, from the church to the court, the judges in red with wigs, led by the chin-up, mace-bearing Town Clerk, and some always rather cheerful, inanely waving, supposedly socialist Lord Mayor. They'd all process in public, at a stately walking pace to the Shire Hall for an assize of trying people. There were some terrible trials. Ah then — when trolleybuses ran and slums were slums: teeming and warmhearted, smoking chimneys, terrible smogs.

And there were black men, from Lagos, Guyana and Jamaica, who'd wear suit, collar and regimental tie and tell you in the public house how they served and fought for *their* Queen in the RAF during the war.

The last vestige of the black Yank lingered, taking a lower and lower profile. They didn't have the flashy car, but a Volkswagen. On the corner where I had my room was a small hotel with rooms to let by the hour to the last of these American soldiers and airmen. There was a horsehair sofa, cardboard boxes stacked in the hall with cans of what comes from Milwaukee brought from an American PX store 100 miles away by this last vestige, who smooched to an old Nat King Cole record with the last of the local floozies.

There are of course American soldiers and airmen in Britain today. But you never see them at all — not in the cities. Then they were just fading away as provinciality began to become proud.

Workers and artists

No one wanted to go to America any more. Our own country was going to be the place. Northern British working class feature films were made. Kitchen sink. Social realism: released and seen by packed attentive audiences. We were on the silver screen — our own back streets — and no-one barracked and mimicked through *Saturday Night and Sunday Morning:* we cheered the heroes on. We were the stars. *A Taste of Honey, Room at the Top.* And a playwright called Arnold Wesker had lobbied the Trade Union Congress in 1960 into passing a Resolution 42 that said artists and workers would combine to promote a new revolutionary working class art. It was a great gesture of solidarity, a new renaissance: trade unions would be the new patrons of the arts.

In 1962 Frank Cousins, Ted Hill, John McGrath, Jennie Lee, Doris Lessing, Alun Owen, Jeremy Sandford et al, led by Arnold Wesker and their friends Malcolm Arnold, John Berger, Sidney Bernstein, Lord Briginshaw, Robert Bolt, Graham Greene, Jack Hylton, Cleo Laine, Compton MacKenzie, Richard Marsh, Spike Milligan, Laurence Olivier, John Piper, J.B. Priestley, Terence Rattigan, Herbert Read, Micky Sekers, C.P. Snow, Ken Tynan *et al*, produced a magnificent manifesto: *Centre 42: the first stage in a cultural revolution.* It is a remarkable document, appealing for donations, and criticising the materialistic world while aiming to change it.

We want all the people to have the chance to enjoy the beauty and riches of life in all its forms. Too much that is good is being cheapened and vulgarised by the purveyors of mass entertainment. Ralph Bond. Association of Cine and Television Technicians.

Centre 42 will be a cultural hub which, by its approach and work will destroy the mystique and snobbery associated with the arts...

The 42 movement is a bid by a new generation of writers, actors, musicians, painters, sculptors, and architects to place art back into the lap of the community: and turn their art from a purposeless mess into a creative force...

It will be the focus of our finest talents equipped to cover the whole of Great Britain, the industrial and agricultural areas — to find new talent...

In the beginning we will take over a large disused building and build a mobile pavilion to enable us to take our work to other parts of the country...

In the end we shall found our own Centres and gardens in every key city in Great Britain...

The trade union movement is undergoing a great revolution. The ordinary community in this generation is producing its own artists. This is our festival of dance, poetry, theatre, folk song, painting and music theatre. This is the beginning of a nationwide movement. We have created it, we can make it a success...

This is an ambitious and far-reaching venture. Undertaken in a spirit of urgency and desperation and with a sure knowledge that, if we do not succeed, then a vast army of highly-powered commercial enterprises are going to sweep into the leisure hours of future generations and create a cultural mediocrity, the result of which can only be a nation emotionally and intellectually immature, capable of enjoying nothing, creating nothing, and effecting nothing.

We do not imagine that the entire population will flock to wherever we are. The years of divorcement have built strong prejudices and it will take perhaps a generation before a new audience is created. Our society has spent centuries destroying man's natural responses to the arts — a generation is little enough time to repair that damage.

What must take place is the creation of a new and unselfconscious cultural framework into which future generations can grow. This is a task which our government should have undertaken, since it has not, then we — public and artist — must do it ourselves.

There was a photograph of bingo in the brochure: bare boards and a trestle table and ladies in felt hats and mufflers, marking their papers on their handbags with rough wooden pencils. How bingo clubs have improved since then! There was a tour promoted for Wellingborough, Birmingham, Leicester, Nottingham, Stevenage, Leeds, Southend, Cardiff, Norwich *et al.* I said I'd help. Put people up — there wasn't really much else I could do. They wanted to do so much themselves and knew what they were doing. Clive Barker wrote that I'd strengthened him politically, as in a weak moment he'd nearly joined the Labour Party. I was just around.

I'd moved by then from my one room to three rooms opposite a cigarette factory. You didn't need to light up in a morning. Just step outside and breathe tobacco dust like smog. I found a puppy dog outside a chip shop. It spent ages crapping in the morning. I put up Michael Kustow, one of the regimental sergeant-majors of the enterprise, the good tank Revolutionary Art. They were all very busy. They did such a lot of things. Their week in our town opened with poetry and jazz, a concert arranged for exactly the same day and time as the local theatre were presenting their first ever poetry and jazz — and neither would budge their dates. Saboteurs of the revolution, said Centre 42. Outcomers, said the local theatre. There was folk song — Ewan MacColl and Peggy Seeger, banjo and concertina. The Ian Campbell folk group and folk singing in pubs. I liked the idea of folk singing. But when it's organised any strengths and taste seem to crumble, or become indigestible, like eating a cardboard cake. There was an idea that public houses would be lent works of art for their walls, and this would be a workers–artists venture between Centre 42 and a local artists' co-operative. But each had a different idea of the meaning of the words collaboration, worker, artist and art. Did the pictures in pubs ever happen? I think it did but such a hassle. Pity the poor publican. Poets in pubs. Brave Christopher Logue reciting — I never heard Laurie Lee. The jazz band was very good. There was a play specially written by Bernie Kops. It was not all bad, and Mr Wesker and the local Trades Council did lots of useful talking together. It was a great shame only a handful turned up to see and hear the bits and pieces in public halls. I was told the poetry in factory canteens was well attended. The jazz really was; jazz you could dance to. I went to every event I could. The brochures were beautifully produced and inspiring to look back on, more so, than *The New Elizabethan Age* by Richard Dimbleby.

They did another play called *The Nottingham Captain,* about a nineteenth century event when workers rebelled, Luddite like, against some machinery, and announced their intention to overthrow the government. They were promised help from Yorkshire miners and all over. Anyway, their revolution flopped, and some got caught and were hanged and drawn at Derby. Their promise of help, it later transpired, was a trick of government agents. The men were just fed up, and the government spies agitated the poor sods into a criminal act, a trap, a show trial and public execution. What a dreadful business. The play ran at the Co-op Hall. It was the first time I'd heard of such things — though nowadays you get them at schools and on television. They weren't known then. No school taught working class revolt. We needed missionaries from socialist London to teach us our bolshy past. A shame so few turned up.

The Miners' Union donated a lump of coal. It stood in the foyer of the Co-op. It was a very big and dirty lump and you had to walk around it to get into the auditorium, or the cloakrooms for the dance. Centre 42 didn't tour again. I wonder what happened to that lump of coal. It could have been preserved in a museum. The Centre 42 lump. It was a very, very big lump — big as a sculpture.

Mr Wesker came back, one last time, for a one-off event in poetry and jazz — in a hall across the road on the same

107

night a local club was having a special annual jazz bop. How did they do it? It was uncanny. As if some fate deliberately led them to double book, and their revolution was blown out like a surfeit of snuff that got right up provincial noses. Mr Wesker complained when only a dozen turned up. He complained at the apathy of the workers, the bungling by the managers of the Co-op. They wouldn't be told. Both sides: the locals knew the tastes and the crusaders knew their tightness — to bring true socialism and save our people.

Centre 42 went back to London, and eventually took the Round House in Camden Town that made a fantastic name for itself in the 1970s with heavy rock 'n' roll and other things. That's still there, a good place no doubt, but the artists–workers' revolution is not so healthy and that missionary zeal didn't even last one generation.

Socialism and the ghost pub

There was a left wing gang I'd met on the square on Sunday soap-boxing. I began to visit their homes, and in one house a lot of them lived together. There was Peter Price who owned the house. He was downstairs, and left wing in education. He was also a light in CND and a teacher for a living. There was always wine and sometimes whisky. There was a garden, and a swing for the summer. There was Jill and George, or was that later? It was difficult to work out who was living in this nest of Marxist Bohemians and who was just visiting a lot. George was the Anti-Colour Bar Campaign that later became the Afro-Caribbean Social and Artistic Centre. Always guests, and another lodger was a businessman interested in general agitation and the Movement for Colonial Freedom who became my great pal in later campaigns. Bob was manager in a local textile factory — and then there was Ken. Ken Coates was the intellectual leader. Legend said he'd run away from the south to the north, and got a job with the working class in the coal mines. When I met him he was teaching, teaching socialism to pitmen on day release. A member of the Labour Party, he'd risen to be vice chairman of the local party, but he was not on the council. The ruling mediocrity kept him down. They wasn't going to fit up the likes of him with a safe Labour seat. They conspired to make sure that didn't happen. He was able to talk much and do little.

Ken was very busy in the working class movement in other ways. He founded a monthly trade union paper, *Union Voice*. It printed broadsheets to pin on factory notice boards, showing how the rich few milked the poor many. He was co-editor with the then young student intellectual Robin Blackburn of *The Week,* a digest of world revolutionary news for busy socialists. This was all before photoelectric printing so Ken's sheets were hard labour at the duplicator, for all who called on the house to take a hand. There was a third journal — *International Socialist* — done with a union leader. None of them was very amusing and certainly not popular. They hadn't the quality of *Universities and New Left Review.* They printed none of my small pieces. I wasn't that trenchant or significant, and they weren't into youth culture. They were fertilizer for the workers, and their shop stewards: for the class struggle.

When you entered their house, number 54, you entered a world of candlelight, wood fires, bookshelves overfilled with books, floors piled with magazines, and for some reasons — I don't know whose choice it was — Wagner loudly on the record machine. I was fascinated. It was a real political cell, and lifted leeches from beneath my eyes. Number 54 was a meeting ground and talking shop to which all sorts from all parts of the world would come in and go out through the same door with much the same opinions as they went in with — as you do when you go to chapel — only you'd be strengthened. Number 54 was a house of rebels, and none of them a rascal. They were the goodies. The baddies were the ones with power on the Labour Party Executive, and the city councillors who took their seats beneath a Labour banner but were not socialists, and the full-time officials who worked the power house of the local Labour Party headquarters. How could the rebels seize the party machine and make it produce the socialism it was supposed to deliver? They have never had their chance. The tea and toast, beer and good fellowship flowed and the duplicator never seemed to stop. The political battles were real and harsh and never won, so ultimately frustrating. The taking of the party HQ was always in sight, the control of the official machine was always close, but it was like running up a down escalator.

Later Ken teamed up with Bertrand Russell, and when the old philosopher died, they got enough money to go full time and set up a printing works and all sorts of revolutionary socialist enterprise and they do that today.

Quite near to number 54 was the ghost pub. Ghost because its customers had been taken away. A local pub: it had lost its local population. The back streets around it had been pulled down but the pub remained, isolated on a rubble of derelict land. These were the days when liquor licences could be transferred, and brewers feared if they closed the pub and let its licence go they might lose that licence for ever. They were building a new public house somewhere in the suburbs, and would transfer this old licence to that. Until the new was built they would keep this open. The poor old landlord and landlady had to trade as best they could, and that included serving people after hours. Knock, knock on the window pane...

At half past ten the landlord's wife would sift the customers, giving the wink to her favourites, and drink up please to the casual and unwanted. If she couldn't sift without aggravation, if someone was indiscreet, that blew it and we all had to leave. But usually she sifted successfully, and we stayed behind locked doors, easily drinking long after the permitted hours. But one false look, one too smart a word, rub her the wrong way and that would be it. No drinks for anyone. It's way past time, she'd say at two-thirty, come on let's have you on your way. Sometimes there would be a knock knock on the window pane: "Sshh." She'd open the door ajar. "Good gracious, it's Peter Price." And he would enter the salon of spirited socialists with cigars from Havana, and scrap metal merchants without their wives, and the ponce escaping from his neurotic prostitutes, and various literati. We drank mild and bitter, and played dominoes because the landlady liked to play dominoes. People talked across their groups, about life and the world.

The virtue of the number 54 network was I think that it was a network and not a cell or club. Solidarity was a word often used and rarely applied. It was people: any politically left, interested, conscious people, from young nothings like myself to long serving communist cadres who had left the party after the people's uprising in Hungary had been put down by the Russians in 1956. No church people of course, nor teetotals and not many operative or labouring classes. There were Ken the rose grower. Professor John of education and Professor Edward, another academic, in classics. There was Rod, a carpet salesman, and Bob, who became my great pal later on, was just a jolly entrepreneur. There'd be miners and engineers. Some students but not a lot. There were always visitors from abroad. There was David Caldwell and his brother Malcolm who became a great friend of the Vietnamese and died, ironically, after the war with America was won. He was murdered in Kampuchea. There were the Coggan brothers — one was a journalist on the evening paper. We always thought we could get a story filed through him — and the other one he went on to organise PROP, the prisoners' rights organisation. "Sshh." Scratch, scratch at the door. "It's a policeman." Drinks away. Open a jar. "Oh come in, out of the cold," she'd say. "Isn't it raining, Constable, what'll be your poison?" And they did, in the days before personalised radio, when coppers blew whistles.

Ken organised a workers' control conference, and wanted a Saturday night party for the delegates. It was the first post-war conference for socialist workers' control in the factories, and they didn't want a sherry do like CND but a boozing party with a bit of a knees-up. I ran that social — because the ghost pub was much too small I found a big old boozer, and bedecked it with a revolutionary banner and a band. It was the best room in the Boulevard, when it still had marble to lean on, potted palms and cane chairs, and it was smashing.

Ken took me to meet some miners. To look at them. They were a long way away. Ken said they had stoned the Marquess of Hartington when he came to their village as the Tory candidate in the 1945 General Election. Colin MacInnes had written that our world was to be classless, and this land Ken Coates took me to was called the Dukeries, with miners and marquesses and not much in between or other sorts. It all seemed a long way away. There was a shire paper, a thick monthly glossy full of pictures of horses and receptions at stately homes in aid of the Red Cross, and I thought all that was dying away — when a young trendy began a rival "county" monthly magazine, with glossier pictures, more ponies than horses, wine and cheese rather than port, the Rotary rather than the Freemasons' lodge and grinning swinging dollies rather than the tweedy ladies. But they were still having receptions at manor houses in aid of the Red Cross. The new magazine did very well. That county world goes on, like the *Tatler* and *The Field,* it seems for ever — though they say their standards have dropped, hasn't everyone. They are still the upper crust.

Colin MacInnes was wrong about class — the glasses through which he saw the world were London and Colonial turning into Commonwealth, and it may be difficult with that bias and belief and seeing the big world change, British red leaving the map and the superficial changes in our towns. It is difficult to appreciate the unobtrusive strength of the shires. They still own the land, the gentry galloping on, away from town. The country Ken Coates took me to was the world of D.H. Lawrence, described in *Lady Chatterley's Lover,* and it was alive and kicking, and still is: maybe more so than this new world of Blacks and youth Colin described and championed in *City of Spades.*

113

Vote for a madman

A night one April I was in the ghost pub and the number 54 Labour Party rebels were drinking and talking of the impending municipal election. Peter Price was going to stand, but not in a safe Labour district. They kept the safe seats for old faithfuls and party hacks. That's a nice word. A hack is a coughdrop. A party coughdrop. New boys and rebels, however old, like Peter, had to be worn weary, fighting where there was a fight: where they could only win by a miracle. But the swing in '63 was to Labour. Peter was standing in a possibly winnable ward. If only, they said, a Liberal would stand and split the Conservative vote, Peter might get on to the council. If only, they said, one of us was not so involved within the Labour Party. Ray?...

In my pots, Billy beside me said he'd be my agent. In the morning I walked the district and I liked it — to represent the people. The day after I had decided to stand for the election, not to split the vote and help poor Peter, but to have some fun and try myself. It was my time. For a year I'd been living as a passive citizen. Now I knew a little, I'd speak a little. It could shake people up a bit. Tradespeople, and people in the pub supported me or said they did — but when does a shopkeeper ever disagree with a customer about the weather? Nippy this morning: certainly is. Bright today: lovely. And why not — if numbers of people at a wedding reception all pat you on the back and say you're a jolly good fellow, don't you become a jolly good fellow? I was going to stand. I was going to make an impression. This was before Screaming Lord Sutch stood at Stratford upon Avon after the fall of Mr Profumo. I was a pioneer. I sat down and wrote my manifesto and I meant every word. Reading it back, it is embarrassing. I should have been full of grand gestures of peace and love, but hippies and ecology hadn't been

114

invented then and I was just parochial. I was conscious it was a local election.

Standing for public office was exciting. Coming out and seeing your name on the posters — and it was so easy. I needed no money in advance: no deposit. And doing it I gained friends. To begin with I read a Labour Party booklet on how to get yourself nominated. It was an atlas I didn't need, for I found a compass through a sea of red tape in a nice girl in the Town Clerk's offices. She thought it was fun: the first screwball she'd had — and when you're fun and new you can do anything. My first nomination paper had to have twelve signatories of registered electors, people who don't necessarily agree with you but sign to say you are who you are, and it is a genuine stand. I got acquaintances in pubs to sign. Shopkeepers wouldn't: "Oh I do agree with you, but being in trade I couldn't put my name to anything." Publicans wouldn't. I found most of my acquaintances weren't registered to vote, when I took my forms in they were wrong. The girl sent me out with another and an exact list of voters, and I got all the signatures right, but some signed "Ray" instead of "R.A." as it said on the list and the names had to be exactly the same, precisely as they were on the list.

Now that girl in the Town Clerk's office, she could have merely done her duty. Taken my form and said she'd pass it on and I'd be informed. By the time I was informed it would be too late. But no — this girl went through the signings with me, there and then. She sent me out again, pressing me to do it quickly and educated enough so this third time I did know A from a bull's foot and, I got it right — just in time, with her help. With the correct papers she trundled me into the Assistant Town Clerk's office, I think with Billy my agent, and he inspected formally, frostily. Then he trundled me into the man himself, the Town Clerk, who stood up and shook hands, and said all in order, jolly good, signed and sealed, you are nominated, jolly good show, play fair, square, into your corners and come out fighting clean, shake my hand, again, I wish you well. Smile. Goodbye.

I was standing as a loony. I didn't call myself loony officially. I wasn't that honest or brave or certain to begin with. I was frightened that calling myself a madman might upset people. I did want to do well. I was frightened of scoring two figures, or maybe no-one would vote for me but myself. You can vote for yourself. I called myself "Independent Liberal". I still thought, as the 54 gang suggested, that with this tag I might pull Liberal votes. It was in the evening papers: "Last minute surprise nomination." And a picture of me — Liberal. The next day I was visited by two persons. Mick put the Alsatian into the bedroom, and showed them into the other room. It stank of Pompadour hair lacquer and bacon. You could hear girls giggling through the plywood partition. "Em, em, uur," the two persons said, they didn't want tea or coffee or *anything* to drink. They perched on the edge of the bed-settee. They had upright backs, kept their coats on, and said they were from the — er, Liberal Party. I couldn't get them anything. They hadn't known me, you see. Forgive them, but... em, how exactly was I a Liberal?

At first they were persuasive: would I like to join the Liberal Party? They then became hurt and puzzled. I must see that I must retract. I did see that? They had to dissuade me from calling myself Liberal. They were more than peeved: they were genuinely hurt — I was abusing their word. It was their word. Finally, they left, convinced I was not their Liberal. On the doorstep their parting shot was: "And I tell you this, you'll be barred from the Liberal Club for life."

I held a press conference. That is, I typed a note, and put it in the letterbox of the morning and the evening paper, the radio station and the television company, I waited at the arranged time in the ghost pub and nobody turned up. But the next day, papers I hadn't written to like the *Daily Sketch* and the *Daily Mirror* printed nearly an inch of the story. "Vote for a madman. Just for once in

116

your life, vote for a madman. I am not your honest politician. I am not sane. I'm not honest. I'm not rich. I'm nothing..."

We had two versions of the leaflet printed. They were the same except one had an X at the top and the other a picture of me with me collar turned up and a fag in me gob. We distributed them in alternate houses: the idea being that the noticeable difference would provoke curiosity and encourage them to be read. Such trust in neighbourliness proved to be unfounded. People who lived next door to one another in neighbourly working class districts frequently did not speak to one another, not even the "Good morning, Mr Hart," of my father on his bicycle, tingaling.

We distributed the manifesto. Everywhere. Fly posted; put it in letterboxes, left copies on pub tables. Everyone said they were ever so interested. I wore the same clothes every day. In the ward the nippers were squealing behind me: "Here comes the madman, mam."

I always had a pal with me. Billy my agent could never find the time, so anybody had to do. Strangers pulled out of pubs. Follow me. "I feel lonely doing this on me jack. Hold this bundle." You must never be on your own. I couldn't say of myself — I am the madman. Somebody had to do it for me, so they could add in a whisper: "Daft as a brush is he, or a new broom? Think where the same sane ones have got us."

My manifesto continued: "I have nothing to lose, no reputation, no business, no property — and I can afford to say just what I please. A council wouldn't work at all with many madmen — but without one or two fearless little..."

We held a meeting. People remembered. Their Chief Constable, Captain Athelston Popkess had investigated a Labour alderman who built a garage to his home, using council cement. The Captain had had to be investigated for investigating. People remembered the councillor who nearly bought a planetarium, with our money, from East Germany and was stopped in the nick of time. People

117

remembered the Tories who stopped the building of a new theatre when it was half built, so that it cost more to stop building than it would to have kept the building rolling. I said in my manifesto: "I can promise little but to act as a catalyst, to shake up — ginger up. Chance a loony."

Meanwhile, the two big political parties were locked in an earnest battle. The Conservatives, "sound and solid", had hiked council house rents for those who could not prove they were in need. If you proved you were poor and needy, you could use a rent rebate scheme, and pay less. The Labour Party said — Means Test: a vicious interference into the private lives of the poor. The Tories had tried to sell council houses to sitting tenants, and in three years had managed to sell only twenty-four from a stock of thirty-four thousand. My Tory opponent, Mr Gough, had been a newsagent and was now selling motorcar tyres. He was a Rotarian and said if elected, we will convert city streets from being gaslit to all electric. The Labour promised they would appoint a city architect. If only we had known... Labour produced a newspaper with a message from their leader, Harold Wilson:

> *Labour will seek to build up Britain's moral strength in the things that count,*
> *1. Social security.*
> *2. Clear the slums.*
> *3. Protect the consumer.*
> *4. A root and branch reform of our education system, to give real opportunity to our young people.*

How could anyone compete with that? Lord Richard Marsh had added, "Let us sweep poverty into history," and my pal Peter had written his own little personal extra bit: "I am a Socialist. Spend no more money on wars... Five million workers are earning less than £5 a week. Look around," wrote Peter, "you are citizens of one of the richest countries on earth — does it look like it? The people of this neighbourhood make the goods which make the money. Looks like somebody else spends it for you..." There was an advert for shopping at the Co-op, and buying the *Sunday Citizen,* and paying sixpence a month to join the Labour Party. I felt ashamed, standing as a loony against all that.

Voting day came, and that morning's *Manchester Guardian* carried a feature on half a page by Stanley Reynolds, "Like mad", with a picture of me. We'd killed any hope of kidding anyone that I was anything but a young, naive non-aligned stirrer-up. What's wrong with that? — the Liberal Club had already barred me for life.

The rest of my household were hung over and asleep, even on that day. I was up early on my own, trudging the streets, and for the first but not the last time being saluted by policemen. The Tories were about in cavalcades at every booth, with wives and cousins and aunts in hats. I was catching the bus from polling booth to polling booth. No idea how many votes we were catching, or where they were coming from. At six, or maybe before, I retired in defeat, with the blues to bed, but at seven suddenly we had an army of supporters pulling people out of pubs and that lifted me. We were in for a revival. Two cars and a van — the coffee bar set to the rescue — at last there was optimism. Miney was there and Courtenay and the Ponce bought us drinks in the pub. Back round the houses we went and we could have carried on all night. It was over at nine.

Making a name
for yourself

At about eleven o'clock the results were declared in a school hall.

J. Gough (Conservative / Tory)	*2511*	*53%*
P. Price (Labour / Socialist)	*1687*	*36%*
R. Gosling (Independent / Loony)	*475*	*11%*

There had been a poll of 41 per cent of the electorate and the campaign had cost me £36. The Tory made his victory speech: clean fight, and best man wins. The Labour candidate said: thank you Mr Returning Officer and your staff, clean fightish. We'll fight again and next time win. Cheers from his supporters — and then the eyes of the counting room turned towards our trestle table. I couldn't face it. We rose and muddled out: bad losers.

And was it worth it all? Oh yes — a spanner thrown to the people and a story to tell. The next night I went to London and appeared on the television as a sociological freak. They paid my train fare and I'm certain a fee of exactly £36. I made enough from the appearance to cover the costs of my election campaign. "Whether they won or lost in yesterday's local government elections," said Cliff Michelmore, "there is no doubt that all the candidates presented themselves to the voters as responsible and level headed leaders of the community, all eminently sane: all except one candidate."

Vote for a madman, said I, just for once in your life, vote for a loony. And then another telly face, Brian Redhead, said how I had lost *(aahr),* and I spoke some more words of my own manifesto, having to read them from a written card, I was so nervous in the heat of studio lights. I read: "A council couldn't work at all with many madmen, but without one or two fearless little creatures, it'd all get too big for its boots..." Did I really say creatures? — anyway it went down well. It was good television. Would I stand for Parliament? Be a national loon, now I was quite famous? I'm not so sure, I said like a statesman. National campaigns need a lot more money and you don't necessarily get it back. Others tried it later. William Rushton, the satirist and latter day TV advertiser, lost his deposit against Alec Douglas-Home in West Perth; Screaming Lord Sutch lost his in August that year and polled less than 1 per cent at Stratford upon Avon. But his was a lovely campaign. I went across to help — *Vote Sutch and Gain Much.* Within a decade scores were doing it at every election. Why not promote a lunatic party? Have a madman standing in every ward and constituency? Are there that many attractive loonies around?

Why not run a campaign saying vote for no-one, spoil your ballot paper — don't vote: don't encourage them. This year for a change, mark your ballot paper "Balls to all of you" to show what you think of them, bullshite or cowshite, write in Andy Capp or Just William or Billy Bunter as appropriate. I knew from my election experience that officials, the officers and tender clerks, put all disputed and peculiarly marked voting slips on a spike to be checked in the presence of the candidates and they became most disturbed and hurt to see deliberately spoiled papers. No-one wrote in juicy gossip about the candidates, but there were one or two I saw with "fuck off" scrawled across them — it is a terrible thing for a citizen of a democracy to take the time and trouble to go into a polling booth and write upon the paper as if it was a lavatory wall. Why does it never happen in the Soviet Union? — does it? The point is to shock. It seems to me the right to vote was so hard fought for, it would be a shame to merely abstain. If you don't like any of them, write your feelings on the paper. Spoil it in a positive way.

121

The 54 gang were upset. My standing had not let their man in, and I'd clearly developed some silly ideas — but upstairs in the Kardomah coffee bar I was the hero, the toast of Saturday morning gateaux. In Yates's Wine Lodge I was the recipient of many a leading port for a spoof well played. During the election campaign I had been astounded to have many Bohemian boys and girls say to me that their parents wanted to meet me, usually the stepmother. The idea of standing as a loony had tickled some society people. As the governments of the Western world were later to learn, the threat to their existence comes not from red Russia or downtrodden workers at home uprising, but from their own middle class sons and daughters, often encouraged by a delightfully witty, wilfully naughty aunt. I was the best entertainment they'd had in yonks. Those aunties twinkled at me and I twinkled back. I was welcomed in fashionable and powerful homes like an eighteenth-century Roman Catholic priest. "Don't you dare breathe a word you've been here, because my husband says — d'you know what he says? — he says you are a most obnoxious rat: you should be put down like vermin. He is such a silly man, my husband. I think you are very sweet: carry on. You must carry on. Take this." — and as I was pushed out of the tradesmens' entrance I'd be slipped £5. No one gave me a lot of money, some none, but the encouragement was enormous. Usually it was an assignment set up mouth to ear from the coffee bar crowd, but one man wrote me a letter. "I am over forty and terrified. Between now and the polls I've some time to spare... Behind the scenes... Some of the Tarzans in our political scrub are not going to enjoy the sight of any authentic jungle boy chopping his way in... Can I help?"

When I lost I didn't lose the friendship. I had entrée into a network of supporters of liberal causes: a kind of freemasonry of private backers from within the middle class, from within what should be high Conservative camps. On my own generation's coffee bar circuit I was, of course, a hero. I now cut a figure: an equal among the elite. I'd credentials — a poor boy from out of town. I earnt my recognition: by standing as a loony I'd entered society as a somebody.

During the election I also met a lot of ordinary people of great strength and sensitivity. They weren't going to vote for me, but they wanted to test my sincerity. They said — we'll never see you again: you'll be just another nine day wonder. Just to prove them wrong, I went back, to every one after the election.

There was Wally who lived by Alan Sillitoe's brother, Michael, in a terraced house opposite where I bought my bags of coal. It was called Forster Street after the man who made education compulsory in the nineteenth century. Wally was another ex-communist, though he still took the *Daily Worker,* and together we mourned the passing of the *Sunday Citizen,* the Co-op newspaper. I'd just started to write for it when it closed.

Wally's front room had books — the first time I ever saw Marx and Lenin in an ordinary family front room, as read books, and the first copy of *The Ragged Trousered Philanthropists* I borrowed was Wally's. It's the classic working class political story about conditions for socialism among the workers, who are house painters in Hastings. I've always thought how curiously English that our most revolutionary working class novel should be set in Hastings, rather than Wigan. It's like Engels of Marx and Engels, spending his last years and dying in Eastbourne, having his ashes scattered around Beachy Head lighthouse.

There was another man, an older man who had a grotto opposite the art college downtown. Mr Joseph was his name — and, in this grotto was an underground one man cellar of *kultur.* Mr Joseph was a one man band. He was the inspiration and organisation to this one man arts centre he christened Aladdin's Cave. He did it without subsidy, and he had no patron, nor money of his own. He went out to work I think and opened his cellar in the evenings. There were fairy lights rigged around the entrance like my father handmade for our Xmas tree. Aladdin's Cave was the cellar of a large lodging house, and Mr Joseph duplicated a programme for these grottoes he made of art and magic, advanced and classical thinking. On Mondays it was — I forget what it was. On Tuesdays the programme was something else. He'd welcome anybody's contribution and wanted everyone to take part. He'd put a blackboard on the street, chalking up the artistic dish of the day, like he was advertising steak and kidney pud. (homemade), two veg. (fresh) at a special price for today's working man's dinner.

7.30   Poetry reading from Keats
8.30   Violin sonatas from Mendelssohn
9 pm   Coffee — with cream
9.30   New poems from Nottingham

Aladdin's Cave was a three dimensional Third Programme. Mr Joseph a priest of high culture, a missionary. He was always harassed. What he wouldn't do, if only a foundation would grant him some money. He had plans for extension. Of course his raincoat was dirty and his shoes were down at heel. He was so busy. I would listen to him play the violin, to an audience of two. He was very grateful. "Usually, at these recitals," he'd say, "there's only an audience of one — my wife." His wife did the painting and drawing class, mostly drawing Mr Joseph. And this cellar was right bang opposite the art college, and it was avoided by all art students. Why? Were they not born with eyes? To daily walk past Mr Joseph's Exchange and Mart of Art, and on sunny Saturdays and Sundays Mr Joseph would stand outside and they'd cross the street to avoid him. "Painting class at 3 o'clock. Violin at 7. Puppets tomorrow afternoon, all free at Aladdin's Cave," he'd cry — like he was busking Punch and Judy on the sands. He wrote me a letter recently. He has moved to the seaside, and is doing very well, he says, God bless him, with the puppets in Great Yarmouth and Cromer and Sheringham.

In those days art students looked inside their heads. Gone were the days of looking down at the pavement. It was all the head, or the galaxy beyond the natural order, as politics was Cuba and exploration was the Moon. You wrote on the wall "Babies are dying in Biafra" in blood coloured paint with caring and feeling, yet the crank along the street — you had no curiosity for him. And Mr Joseph wasn't young, or fashionable, or in the know, or part of the college certificate: nor was he being actively oppressed. No-one said "Good morning, Mr Joseph." Tingaling. He was an embarrassing curiosity, not to be encouraged. Interfere in Indo-China, tell the President of America what to do, but you cannot smile at the eccentric old man who lives next door, because he's full of Shakespeare and Mozart in a dirty raincoat. It's irrelevant. The world was going to be changed. Not us. The kids are all right.

Provincial Bohemia

I'd known the private life of Bohemia, of course, before the election. I was happiest there. After the election I had new friends who'd wheedle me introductions to private houses and posh flats. Their encouragement cushioned my electoral failure. If I'd failed to win a seat on the council, I had won an entreée into some amazing drawing rooms. Dowagers and go-getters. Harry was an older man who welcomed the 1960s and had a flat in the centre of town. There was always something to eat, and bookcases crammed with contemporary magazines and books from Jean-Paul Sartre to Joe Orton. No one knew Harry but me. I mean, he wasn't a drinker, or a trader, and I didn't meet him through any political gang. He'd simply approached me at election time. He wasn't on any scene, and he wasn't very interested in me. He was full of himself, just like Colin MacInnes, his doings, his thoughts — "The world, it's all going to end with a bang very soon." — but Harry had that gift of hospitality and of being there I'm not sure anyone has today. There was no catch. "Any way I can be of help... food... telephone... need a rest any time..."

I'd still go to Bohemia, lower Bohemia, but first I'd breakfast with Harry. Before taking on the coffee bars and booze, I'd have a meal. It made a difference. Harry was on a committee that ran an art gallery and he kept the key for them. He was interested in art, theatre, had been in India, been a publican. Saturdays were always nice days but now they developed. Breakfast with Harry. On to the town, and then back to this art gallery which was across the way from Harry's flat. A gaggle of us would haphazardly gather in the gallery, where upstairs was a Sadia water heater. Harry and Mary made Nescafé and if conversation went on, they could lock up when it finished.

This art gallery was rather special. It had begun before my time, founded by a lawyer and his lady who painted. They bought a shop to sell their works, and that of their friends. A shop that would have the highest contemporary standards, and they ran it as an artists' co-operative, in a trust rather than selfishly as a private enterprise. To be a member you had to be an exhibiting painter, sculptor, potter or jeweller and have your work approved by the committee before it could be shown in this gallery.

This was exactly the opposite of a poetry magazine I admired at the time called *Breakthru,* edited out of Haywards Heath by Ken Geering — *Breakthru* published every damn single poem that was sent to it. It just ran them, duplicated every month, no editorial, no selection, everyone equal — that was the way of the 1960s.

The 1950s, when this gallery was started were a much more choosy time; like the Festival of Britain, the gallery wanted only the best, and when the committee met they were expected to have the highest standards, and if no-one met them, they would rather have the walls blank. The committee were all artists, except a laid down few (10 per cent) who could be elected associate members and take part in the general management of the gallery: people who were art-appreciators, writers, teachers, buyers, the lawyer and useful people like Harry. They were fine liberal folk, who had hard opinions about art. They liked modern art. I liked their toughness and it made Saturday a new kind of day.

The location of this gallery was between Harry's flat and the new theatre. It was ideal. Harry could feed me and I could cross and mingle in the theatre bar, which was *the* fashionable place of town. It was new and shiny and had been opened by Princess Margaret's consort, with the Lord Mayor, the Vice Chancellor of the University, the Duke of Portland, and lots of Conservatives and socialists in monkey suits. Herself had had to cry off at the last moment as she was having a baby — hurrah,

hurrah — and sent her regrets with her husband — hurrah. They had come to open (at last) the controversial and plushiest — cost much too much but isn't it all worthwhile now? — civic theatre. They had excerpts from *Coriolanus* by William Shakespeare: the real thing would have been too long. They had their own speeches to listen to as well. Ah, the days when we were proud of our drains, and now were proud of our theatres. This was where on Saturday mornings the in-crowd swung. Ah — those clichés of the day. We didn't use them, but we purred inwardly when we heard people use them about us.

I was elected after a little tussle on to the art gallery committee. Maybe second attempt it was. People often have to say no, at the first. So life was no longer merely swanning through snack bars decorating town with my lip. Now I was "on committee" of an art gallery, I'd a handle to my name. I was an ear to bend. People said: how could I get my paintings hung at your place? People said: that last exhibition was rubbish, whose idea was that? At the committee meetings, there was always a battle royal between the old guard of freelance artists who struggled in a Bohemian way and painted often what they thought their friends would buy. They'd be small pictures, modern as the turn of the century, but figurative and landscapes. There were a lot of good painters, and each one was an individual.

Sitting opposite the old guard was the up and coming, ultramodern trend. They whispered to one another. They were a conspiracy, constructing their reputations out of pure form and mixed media. They offered their works at ridiculously expensive prices, only museums could afford to buy. They didn't want to sell: they wanted the review, the kudos, the reputation was everything. They'd be immaculately turned out: the best frames, best canvas. "They could afford it," the Bohemians said, "they're all college teachers with eight weeks holiday a year, and they get grants, bursaries to America and everything,

128

and now they want to take over this little gallery we've built up." What could be done about it? The new people had higher standards of excellence. They were nice people, but... they just didn't have to struggle with their paintings on the bus.

The gallery had functions. Once a month the exhibition changed and the opening of a new show would be a glittering occasion. Everyone would be there. And on Saturday mornings, almost everyone would gather to discuss the exhibition at length and have a coffee with Mary. Many of those present would be the artists, but the lawyer was a regular. There was a mathematician who owned a sailing yacht. A surgeon — the first doctor I ever met socially — and a Dutch woman who was very modern and much too rational for me. I enjoyed it all, and was invited to house parties with punch and architects, senior civil servants and politicians in power were present. They were just parties. No orgies or anything — just drinking and lots of jaw-jaw.

The gallery eventually moved to a much bigger place, and the old artists lost control to the new teachers and the Arts Council and "statutory bodies". The life I had enjoyed eased away. The new place was in a warehouse district, and near no exciting theatre bar. Anyway, by then the new theatre was no longer new and fashionable. The old guard artists who really only ever wanted to sell their paintings to friends set up small commercial galleries in the suburbs, and in the country villages, or simply sold by telephone. It has all changed — but when I joined, the place was on a knife edge and there was a real dialogue. We talked about modern paintings that were just a single colour on a large canvas with one wavy line across. Was that art? Some of the artists were very deep. Others were simple high energy people, hungry for reputation. Reviews in the *Manchester Guardian* mattered. The committee could be very influenced by what papers like the *Sunday Times* said was modern. They paid attention to pundits, but they were very wary of committing themselves to any local daring. Travelling exhibitions were simply the best of contemporary art, but members' exhibitions were hotly contested. The selection committee deliberated long and seriously in secret session before deciding which of their own pictures were worthy to be hung.

In the basement was a small gallery anyone could hire (committee discretion but not inspection). Older members and students exhibited here, off-beat and smaller one-person shows. It was cheap, worthwhile and unnoticed by the papers unless you advertised it yourself. I helped friends do that. I got Richard Wollheim up: he was a Professor of Philosophy I'd had a public argument with in *Tribune*. He was the first man I ever met with a telephone account at a bookies. You know, he'd lie in bed in the mornings reading the back pages, or the *Sporting Life,* and ring up his turf accountant to place his bets before he got out of bed. I thought that was a marvellous way for a Professor of Philosophy to begin a day. Very royal.

I also had friends of my own age, more interested in fun and games than either form or landscape. Mary who made us coffee encouraged us young ones. She was a shy lady and the general dogs-body to the committee. She opened up and was there every day, appearing in charge. She had beautiful bright eyes, and a real eye for pictures that didn't need the advice of the *Sunday Times.* She also had an ear for the artist, an understanding of the need to furrow your own path. She said very little. She was encouragement, just by being there — always listening with little advice but "Carry on, I'm sure you're doing right." She never said get a proper job. She was gently, simply, genuinely wanting you to fulfil, to develop what-ever was your artistic talent. She was also naturally, and without spite, anti-state. She loved to sell pictures, whisper your name in a buyer's ear. She hated the apparatus of committee and grant, of wheeling and dealing with forms.

I'd a pal I teamed up with of my own age and disposition who was a painter. He didn't work. Said he was a gypsy boy. He lived on his own, owning up to no roots. He'd made a nest for himself in some sacking in an old caravan at the buttercup end of a field of colliery waste, right at the very end of the six-wheel trolley-bus route from town. Day Parsons he called himself. Played a mouth-organ like he was Bob Dylan. He had been a painter of dodgem cars and fairground booths, and he did big pictures on hardboard, boldly and roughly, figurative paintings of young girls but done on a dark green background. We set them up in the basement we hired, on black walls. It was very weird. When you went down you could hardly see the paintings. The committee were very puzzled. They were such clean, bright and rational people, believing in a clean future. Day Parsons upset them, just by his presence, being rough.

I did other things for them. I wrote the introduction to an exhibition of concrete poetry. They liked that. Dom Sylvester Houédard came and stayed with me. They were very impressed: a concrete-poet monk. I organised the security for a heavily-insured American exhibition of Andy Warhol and things. We had to mount guard twenty-four hours a day. There was another young painter who was very good and drank upstairs in the Wine Lodge where the trio played: Donald Chaffin who painted tiny miniatures of pretty things, like Beatrix Potter bunnies and beautiful sailors surrounded by pansies and roses. Would I help him? Yes please. I did. And Mary at the desk encouraged. He was so good and alive and local and sensitive and trying to be an artist with his own life. I sometimes think the teachers on the committee, with some part of their mind or feeling, actually wanted to kill the tradition of the artist who struggles in his garret, doing his thing, and free as a bird, and living by begging and not caring a bugger for all the newfangled systems.

At committee meetings Mary took the minutes. She'd wink whenever I got naughty. Naughty — I use that word

131

deliberately because there was no malice though I tried to turn the teaching trendies against themselves: try to use my tongue, turn the meeting to further the local living talent among us. Not always successfully. Good tries. Some of the committee on a Saturday morning might have a drink later on in the theatre bar, but chicken out of any invitation to go further. Day Parsons was my great boozing pal. He burned fiercely with what is it? — the young artist's dog desire to explode: do something: be: a feeling older than rock 'n' roll. We were both fond of public looning: street performing: stalking with wide strides like two cartoon cats, howling in the market square. We loved arguing, sometimes just fooling around, sometimes seriously, about rock 'n' roll, Gene Vincent, Jack Kerouac, William Burroughs, Jackson Pollock the painter we liked — and that one who dragged naked ladies across paint-wet canvasses. Not so sure about the Beatles, and we were not so sure about Andy Warhol: was it a rip off or just show business?

Day Parsons did another exhibition, in the basement, this time all in silver paper. Little tunnels or things like children's dens or the film set of *2001*. I thought it was super. The committee all shook their heads, and it had cost a lot of money we'd borrowed and never gave back. We looned around together, maybe two years, decorating the town with our lip. And then Day Parsons went away one day with a beautiful, silent, French girl and never came back.

I remember we went to a local writers' circle, an ancient earnest circle of amateur scribblers, some of whom had stories published in *The Lady* or sold, they said, to New Zealand. They met monthly, and read one another's works out loud. We'd fart and belch. They didn't like politics or sex or four letter words. They didn't know of Mr Burroughs, or the Olympic Press though they liked John Braine and Colin Wilson and Stanley Middleton because they were personalities who'd written raw provincial books, but wore cardigans rather than leather jackets. So prim — we became like snarling dogs in the company of a field full of rabbits. You didn't have to do much but lean forward and breathe on the backs of their necks. They were so kind but with no ideas and no standards and no belief. Some of them were useful for lending you money. Aubrey had no money. I liked Aubrey. He was more indigenous than the rest, untidy and un-rich, but he simpered to all the ladies in hats. Why wouldn't he stand up and speak the poverty and desperation in him rather than up-chinning to these writer-housewives who were in awe of every law and every magistrate that had ever breathed? I took the piss out of Aubrey. I wish now I hadn't. He was a sensitive man. What did he write? I don't know. He did a duplicated magazine. Were his pieces ever published in the local paper? — rarely. If in the revolution we had taken over the local paper, would we have published any of Aubrey's stories? No — the gap between the generations was a swift flowing river, and they were too old, their bones too stiff to cross. We'd no inclination to build bridges.

Our Aladdin's Cave

I was teaching one day a week at the Tech college, I don't know what good that did — liberal arts to engineering students — "Today we'll talk about drugs, next week we'll talk about sex" — but we both enjoyed it, quite a lot for a little while. Opening the eyes of people: everyone should know. 1964 was a good year for students. They were having a radical season at the university, and a deputation of bright boys and girls came to see me and took me out and flattered me up. Would I write for their magazine? When the young flatter those a little older it is irresistible, and the magazine was spectacularly good — for two seasons.

They had another idea: "a splendid idea", I wrote at the time, "has arrived from the Students' Union. They're coming out of their campus on the park and thinking of building a Students' Union type of building in the heart of downtown, for all young people, open to everyone with bars and rooms and corridors: a place where we could put the sixties together: a living magazine, a house for kindred spirits, refuge for minorities, arts laboratory, agitator and spearhead of all the new waves."

It could be exciting. We all envied the Students' Union with their own building out on the campus, full of activity, with its halls and crowded noticeboards, unlocked rooms and careless caretakers, though why did they have epaulettes on their overalls, and rooms marked "committee"? We'd do better if it was all of us, students and non-students: have the hell's angels do the patrolling. This could be *the* place. "It could even happen," I wrote. "This town is jumping out all over, but like self-contained cells, like flower beds on traffic islands: most of the time we don't know what the other pieces are jumping around with — nor they you. If only it could be put together."

Put all the flowers in what a park of promise. I'm not sure now it was such a good idea and what a thought for an anarchist to put everything together — but there it was. A Centre 42 without the boring trade unions. An Aladdin's Cave of our culture. Like the ICA, founded in 1968 in The Mall. What the Beatles did briefly with Apple in London — peace and love and new creation and community profit.

And I thought of those hell's angels patrolling the corridors. And I thought of the building the Russians gave to Warsaw — a palace of culture? I suspected students. Was it a wrong idea? That life needs shelter in buildings: that forces must be organised to increase. I thought of the Mechanics' Institute. Now it was the students' turn. They could begin as the Mechanics of 1860 — how marvellous were their institutes when dreamt: a library for their working class elite; a literary and philosophical society; a scientific and experimental institute; and now it is the club steward and a bar committee rather than a librarian and a laboratory.

I thought of the Co-op, why are their buildings so ugly? I thought of the demise of my own youth club — hell's angels patrolling the corridors. But it was the students' turn: it was a students' world.

A few years later when students didn't seem to have put it together, Geoffrey Cannon got me involved in a strange and speculative scheme called Shantasea in Birmingham. They wanted a junction box of live wires built into a new multi-storey building with recording studios, video, boutiques, and youth culture for everyone. I went to a couple of meetings as an adviser. It was all very high powered: I don't know what became of it. There was going to be a chain of these new age buildings for the alternative culture was upon us — wine bars, art galleries, delicatessens, sex shops, pirate radio on the roof above the planetarium, foreign film clubs in the base-ment and teen canteens and motorcycle repair workshops for the bike boys and to be — *the* place. Shouldn't we have

135

ten-pin bowling in the basement? That was the latest fad. "What about ice skating?" somebody said, as we sat around one of those big shiny tables — ice skating? It was like someone said Terence Rattigan is a writer.

There were books and magazines you could only buy in special places, lots of little magazines from Greenwich Village, New York City, and all over the English-speaking world. Stuart and Martin who drank in Yates's Wine Lodge and listened to the trio with us were teachers. They went part-time and opened an avant garde bookshop, the first of its kind in our town to sell these free-thinking books. Then, with some political elbow, they got a profitable schools' contract for selling text books in bulk. One of them packed up teaching and went full time. They published a magazine. Sponsored poetry readings. Could they get the bookshop in the university? They never got that. Later they went bust. It was very sad. I still owe Martin some money.

All over Britain people were at it. Boutiques were followed by bookshops, and wholefood shops. Sugar, brown sugar and spice, and all things nice, all over Britain. Little people making the alternative society — for art and love and communality. Houses of art and delight, little magazines, alternative press, virgin apples, village lights, grass roots and duplicators for anyone to use. Artistic access for all: the new renaissance.

At every level I was involved — with Alan Horsfall in a "buggers' club" at Burnley: the opposition was outrageous. Gay clubs just didn't exist at that time except at discreet and hypocritical ghettoes. We wanted in Burnley a place, open and co-operatively run where homosexuals could meet with pride, and bring their lovers and their brothers and their mothers and drink and dance together. We approached the churches. They said what you people want is a house in the country, away from the towns, where you can be isolated and helped. We didn't want that. We didn't want just a disco either or a cruising room. We wanted like the

Mechanics' Institute: a little library and a stage for performing plays.

We found some premises ourselves, and agreed a lease. We'd applied for and got planning permission, and a brewery to help pay to convert the premises, but when we went to sign the lease the Co-op, who owned the building, said they'd changed their minds. The signing was supposedly a formality, but the Co-op, we discovered, had pressure brought to bear upon them, as democratic institutions can, from members of their board who'd been got at by the Transport and General Workers' Union who'd been got at by the Catholic Church. And that powerful combination proved fatal.

The Co-op said they wouldn't let the building after all. They were sorry. We said we'd sue. They said go on then. We raised a hue and cry. We called a public meeting in, I think, the town hall. Posters covered the town. And the meeting was packed. The priest came to denounce us, and he did. The local lads turned up for the occasion, and the police made them take off their Doc Martens — or is it Bob Martens — those big red boots they had. The boots were all lined up on the steps outside, and the bovver boys only let in in their stockinged feet. Lots of thinking townspeople turned up — "In their opinion..." they'd begin sentences. "They could be wrong, but in their experience..." By the end of the meeting, everyone except the priest agreed we'd been badly treated and old ladies stood up ashamed of their town, and ashamed of the Co-op and the priest and wet-eyed with admiration for our guts, and wishing us well. But we never got that building.

I remember on another level, in our town, the architects and builders together set up a Design and Resource Centre: this was a new building to house the latest technology so that it could be examined by people. It wouldn't sell anything, but it would advise and display the newest materials, and stage exhibitions of all the latest methods. It did well. They had a little cinema. Coffee too, and wine at opening dos. Technical events but

137

everyone went along. They had the first photostat machine the public could use. I used it a lot. Our Rob worked there on Saturdays and he didn't charge me. It's all gone now. It didn't last. It's been taken over by the Council Planning Department, just used as offices, and, the top floor is a council staff or union employees club. I've never been in it and they say it's quite nice. I don't want to go. I liked it how it was and I want to remember when it was stacked with hundreds of bricks of different shades and thousands of paint and print patterns, and thicknesses of glass and strengths of plastic. There was a paint mixing machine. It was there I saw my first micro-wave oven and gadgets galore — and the man in charge was an enthusiast for life, interested in an open society and the new world, and amateur dramatics as well and all ideas.

Orgies and abortions

In the winter-time of 1964 I first talked to architecture students. They were attached to the art school, so they lived in town, and on town rather than in the university park campus. Change was afoot. This was to be the last year of that arrangement, of architecture as a branch of art. Soon they were to be sent to the campus, but for then, at that time, they were living in town and met monthly in a room above the rowdy, randy students' pub on the Market Square. I was their invited speaker. We drank, and then I talked. I said what I'd done when I ran my youth club — and other ideas of gang enterprise. I went on to divide the world into activities that were either an orgy, a crucifixion or an abortion. Students love classification. For some reason I gave this part of the talk a title — I called it "The Darkness of Virtue" because I think I was reading Jean Genet at the time and that was affecting my style of things. The darkness of virtue: every cloud has a silver lining; every disinfectant smells. Put an idea in a building and it must sink like the Co-op. Defend freedom and, you use the weapons of the bully. Each man kills the thing he loves, said Oscar Wilde.

I began quoting D.H. Lawrence again. From *Nottingham and the Mining Country,* he wrote lambasting us: "The English are town birds, through and through, today, as the inevitable result of their complete industrialisation. Yet they don't know how to build a city, how to think of one, or how to live in one."

Sienna, he went on, returning to this theme again and again, Sienna is but a snip of a place yet it is more of a town than Nottingham. Compared to the Italians or Greeks, we English have been late developers of cities, and yet we have even less city sense than the Americans. And as city-zens we are undeveloped and stupid.

139

Writing of the road from Alfreton to Ripley in Derbyshire, Lawrence cries out: "These mining villages *might* have been like the lovely hill towns of Italy, shapely and fascinating." He's right — rather than follow the contours, we've tried to fight them: tried to better nature. We have blotted our beautiful countryside with an unbearable ugliness, and we have nailed our towns to a cross and crucified their life.

Oh, I think Lawrence was ever so right about England — but the awfulness, the ugliness he so condemned, we have grown accustomed to and sentimental about. For many years since I first fell for Lawrence, out of school, I've been troubled by why it is I feel comfortably smug about the ugliness and meanness he condemned. When I travel down the Erewash Valley that hasn't changed much since Lawrence's day, I don't feel that it's awful in Lawrence's way. In fact my heart beats faster, my stomach stirs, my eyes moisten and I am genuinely excited, singing "Jerusalem" or "Land of Hope and Glory" at the back of my head. Were we not the first industrial nation? Don't we wear our scars with pride? — let us show them proudly. They are scars of honour. And our mean little homes with privet hedges, are we not a private people? Were we not scoffed at by Napoleon for being a nation of shopkeepers? We are untidy because we do a bit of everything: this and that and racing pigeons, growing spinach. I am excited: right proud on a journey that so sickened Lady Chatterley and made the sensitive Mr Lawrence beside himself with fury. And how I've always loved those lines of W.H. Auden. Romantic claptrap I know them to be.

> *Tramlines and slagheaps, pieces of machinery,*
> *That was, and still is, my ideal scenery.*

My heart has lifted up when I've seen from the train, Barnsley and Wigan and Wolverhampton, those bastions and bulwarks of coal: stamping, thumping power, brass bands and giant marrows. They call the Co-op in Barnsley the Barnsley British Co-op. Tombstones in the history of the oppressed that make monumental almost immovable noises in the heads of those like me who feel romantic for the common people. The view through the train of pit heaps, or of ashfields from the top of a trolley bus, in the fog looking down on gaslit streets, slowly and silently moving through a manufacturing district, the Victorian canyons of warehouses and looking up the steep hillsides of a cobble-streeted slum — I feel romantic. And I tell you I would rather that teeming cauldron of backstreet life than the tundra of an overspill estate you reach by motorbus; one of those motorbuses with an engine at the back and a limited fare that crosses the river, beyond the power station, over flat reclaimed land and grey grass roundabouts, lit by orange sodium flares and surrounded by sweeping asphalt roads; at the periphery, with every home hedged in with privet and served by the mobile fish and chip van. They make me want to crawl into a hole and give up. What would Lawrence have thought of them? Progress — we have regressed. These estates are not even ugly. They have no character, as they have no work and the churches on council house estates have no graveyards. They are a bloodless abortion. This is what we're doing: partitioning life so that it becomes a non life.

The slum is awful but it has a purpose, it is a something, as a crucifixion is an event. An abortion is a nothing: a non event. You don't have a service to celebrate, to give thanks or to mourn an abortion. Not even in modern South Bank religion. But a crucifixion makes a religion — there is a ritual to it.

There may be no meaning to it, but there is an order, a purpose, a pattern out of which, as in death, there is comfort. The magic of darkness. And so we (I) can turn our crucified towns, on wicked rainy days, like Bilston and Bacup, Blackwood and Ilkeston into a romance, tragic and solemn, merry and bright notwithstanding the ugliness. A crucifixion is a world that can be so black that when a break comes, a tear of goodness, it shows. When God pricks the black out, the light can be so bright, angelic, pure, white, innocent, wise and beautiful. Slums have been noted as milky ways of good company, of comradeship, life and laughter, with real people, helping hands in times of trouble.

A crucifixion is a grand anachronism: an event or a place so ugly and horrible that it gains a gripping fascination. It fills the eye and moves receptive organs. Life in it is bleak for, however many stars of goodness, no milky way ever shines like the sun. Stars only shine because of the darkness. A crucifixion is like the Church of England prayer book used to be — during a service, moving and emotional and they let you say "Amen" at the end of the vicar's prayer.

A crucifixion is a graveyard service, the rough and tumble of working in a factory; death; black blood; Dracula; the formal dance; the narrow canyons of a manufacturing district or the City of London, with workrooms between the monumental tombstones — *in memoriam;* the sweatshops of Queen Victoria's reign; the reasons for Karl Marx, like Scrooge, Dickensian — and if you cleaned its buildings would they not fall apart? The Ritz, a grand hotel, a very posh district, a Mayfair of rich folk, of villas in mock gothic glory, private roads and pomp, hypocrisy and poverty. The *Tatler, The Field* and *The Gun.* A Rutland flat hat. The foxhunt; a backyard knife fight; the formal restaurant meal. A mug in the greasy spoon transport café; a pawnbroker. A boarding house breakfast at Blackpool; the stock exchange. *Coronation Street;* a gentleman's smoking room club. The entire nineteenth century; the pub wedding party. Pit tips at Gedling; untidied heritage; Liverpool. The Trip to Jerusalem; traditional bookshops; backstreet life. *Steptoe and Son* — I would later have added Alf Garnett and Enoch Powell. Indoor public baths. The bell on an alarm clock.

All these have style and simply understood purpose, and manners to their purpose. You feel that if you hate them, they will hate you back. They make you feel something. As they go, as they're pulled down, everybody comes to love them and to feel slushy affection at their passing. As they're done away with, modernised and made with it, we prize our crucifixions: with all their faults, all the misery they caused, they were as much our history as the palaces of the Czars, preserved by the Soviet Russians.

Thank God Lawrence didn't live to see our modern world of neutered non-events and plastic non-life. We have exchanged the animal for the vegetable for the mineral. Exchanged the crucifixion for an abortion.

An abortion is tasteless, has no smell because the room's anaesthetised. You can't hate it, you can't love it, to anyone with any sensibility or spunk in them, it passes all feeling: it is mind blowing, takes you out of yourself, beyond hate and love. It has no aesthetic, it is an anaesthetic. It is a promise that is not made by a man at whim or of good heart, but by a committee for public good and sensible reasons: it can never be fulfilled because no-one is going to fulfil it.

It is giving a man a bath, a toilet, hot and cold, central heating, television, and taking away his freedom without putting him in prison. Today we have the technological, scientific and human resources we need to make our lives more exciting, more free, full and happy than they have ever been. And no Big Daddy — no need for the rich man to overlord you from his castle the gentleman is defunct. We are all equal. Life can be smooth. We shall neuter industrial horrors and call work play.

In place of the crucifixion we have the gas chamber. In place of the hanging, an injection: one little prick you won't hardly feel and Fido can be put down. They are poisoning our precious bodily fluids. With fluoride they're interfering with us. To make us healthy, they are sapping at our magical powers, closing up the village fountain and the

143

muscles of our soul are growing slack. We all laughed at that general who said in *Doctor Strangelove,* it's not fluoride they're putting in the water, it's a bromide of the soul. There is a truth somewhere in all of this. Our towns are becoming places where we meet only by design. There is little accident, little haphazard or chance encounter. We're becoming so we don't have to touch or smell each other. A city without crucifixion or orgy: without either purpose or meaning of a kind that can be immediately understood. Castrated of any spontaneous excitement, any love by people across section lines. This is what I call an abortion: a non-life. It is as modern as the hour. It is the suburban, the division of humanity into private lives that began with the middle classes in the 1920s and now sprawls across the land and across all classes: a numbing and stunning of all instantaneous human heart and spirit. A neat and packaged life where disturbance is a crime. Bohemian life, of course, but as in a zoo. And a part of town for Teddy boys, and a part for lawyers to work in, and the arts centre and the nature trail. Numbered footpaths for ramblers. The countryside for pensioners' charabancs. And the upper crust, in their black Mercedes, never holiday at home. Once upon a time we all went to church together. Now not even that. We have ceased to be city-zens.

This numbing, stunning — this abortion — happens in clean convenient little homes, for the sake of tidiness. Most English *men,* said Lawrence, loathe the little home: prying, jealous, petty, private: it is the women who love it.

An abortion is a clean kitchen. A new town. Police panda cars. A supermarket. The overspill estate. Food untouched by hand. Good television. Chinese restaurants. Suburbs. Coventry precinct. Industrial museums. Muzak in the crematoria. Preserved heritage. The milk bar. Billy Butlin. Net curtains. Hire purchase. A bypass. The lido. Love with a contraceptive sheath. The Soviet Union. The architecture of the Co-op. A motorway caff.

These notions are only notions. They're not a truth but a party game. Orgy, crucifixion and abortion — and then like the invention of purgatory I thought of a fourth category: of "Bedlams". These are things that are too mad, too crowded, too busy to ever see clearly, like... today I suppose if I was silly enough to continue this game I'd put down discos as bedlams. Then I'd put the ice-rink, Woolworth's on Saturday, a coach station on a Bank Holiday, tea in a crowded department store, the queue in the corner shop on Christmas day, an indoor market, university park on admission day, the traffic jam at a municipal crematorium, as opposed to walking to the graveside.

I'm not sure about bedlams. I think it was just a note. I don't think I ever spoke about bedlams. Maybe all I said was life should be fun and let ourselves be open. Fill all your holes fabulously, said Mr Genet. There can be no code of rights, no bill of liberties. What life should be is an orgy. An orgy is the life of an English gentleman in the eighteenth century. Tom Jones and good Queen Anne. An orgy is infectious: everyone joins in. You do the hokey-kokey and you shake about. The whole of the eighteenth century. The night Forest won the cup. (Until the police arrested H.H. — that was a crucifixion.) Disco dancing when it's gone a little wild. The Wine Lodge on a Saturday when the trio plays. A pub crawl. The piano at the back bar of the Napier. Mr Jackson, the grocer's shop on Piccadilly. A delicatessen: an old open market square: a coaching inn: Goose Fair: Christmas: Lyon's tea shop: Woolworth's normally: an Indian restaurant because you get some taste: a hot sensation: Petticoat Lane: Sneinton Market: fast trains with buffets: Skegness on Bank Holiday: The cremation of Nehru.

I wrote Coventry Cathedral — I don't think I'd put that in now. I wrote all-night laundromats and ten pin bowling — they've proved to be more ephemeral than grafitti — and I included the lower floor of my central Co-op store because at that time it combined a smart shirt counter, a book and magazine shop, a record browserie and, on a slightly higher level, an American bar where

145

they served long, shocking pink sundaes and you could view everybody.

An orgy is an event, a fiesta, something fabulous. (How awful those words were to become.) We have yet to learn, us English, that pleasure is to be taken. Every freedom we have is licensed, and we worry if to enjoy ourselves is in order. Licences are abortions.

If abortions are things you think twice about, then it's cerebral and too late to feel any surge of feeling. An orgy you just do, do it because it feels good — a common stomping ground in a public place, where you can take part or be a spectator. For all classes without being classless, or anonymous. The most difficult trick for English life to perform. A place with taste, not afraid to give offence but quick to turn offence with wit. A melting pot: would the students' building downtown be like that? Or would it be an abortion? A mirage. It would not be a crucifixion — be sure of that. A crucifixion is a negative and nobody builds crucifixions today. Everybody wants to be positive, participatory — no-one believes in evil — but an orgy is the sun.

Buckminster Fuller

At the end of my talk the students said come here and we became pals; we talked and they took me back with them. I'd be in their company a lot. I became their H.H. — a slightly older, sometimes silly, pet genie, camp follower mascot at their parties. Not often is there that response after a talk to students, but this time a relationship developed. Like lending someone a book so often, they don't even bring it back. Sometimes though, when they bring your book back, they bring along one of theirs to lend to you. A kindred spirit. A gift to say thank you, for one good turn deserves another. In appreciation. That's what happened. I lent Paul Goodman and got back Samuel Smiles. I lent Colin MacInnes and got back Jane Jacobs. George Orwell/Arthur Koestler came back. Christopher Alexander. My collection of *Anarchy* and they said we'll take you to hear R. Buckminster Fuller. There were no books of Bucky Fuller at that time, but Bucky was on a world talking tour in 1965. He was a guru before that word was in currency, before Timothy Leary and the Beatles in India were fashionable. Mr Fuller was an American designer–inventor. He came to our town for a one night stand at the new architecture tower in the university park. I was mesmerised. Not since Billy Graham had I been so moved by a speaker to do something, to personally let his force enter my life. We sat in tiers as in a cinema. The lights dimmed and this man in a smart business suit stepped briskly to a spotlight lectern. He put his fingers to his large bald head and closed his eyes.

"When I was a little boy. Can you hear me?"

"Yes," we shouted back.

"When I was a little boy," he was speaking very fast, "I'd go to church with my mother and my mother brought me home one day. There was an uncle I had not seen sitting at home. This uncle took me into the study, said 'Sit down boy'. I sat down and my uncle said to me: 'Boy, I'm going to tell you the facts of life, you're grown up enough now. Not many people know about the facts of life. It's a good thing you go to church with your mother, but never forget these facts of life. You listen to me. In England a long time ago there was a man who was a scientist and Malthus was his name. He was the first man to have in front of him all the facts about all the world. He looked at these facts. He saw there was not enough to go round. Well, he told his employers, the East India Company, and they said, this is dangerous information. You'd better keep it very quiet. It's on the secret list. Because if everybody knew there was not enough to go round they'd be fighting all the time. It's a good thing people go to church and pray and hope and believe God will provide. But God is not going to provide because he can't, that's what Malthus discovered. Now, boy, I don't want to disillusion you. It's a good thing you going to church with your mother, but you remember what I told you. In this world there's not enough to go round. We got some: your family have, so don't go giving it away."'

And Buckminster Fuller opened his eyes. He looked at us. No one clapped. We just looked at him. He then put his fingertips back on his bald head and I thought, you look like a cross between that Yul Brynner and the Mekon who was the supercreature in the *Eagle* comic strip. He continued, short sentences at a rapid rate of knots.

"After Malthus came Darwin. You all hear of Darwin with the theory of survival for the slickest fittest and most people believe this to be true today but it is not true. Malthus is wrong. Darwin is wrong. There is enough to go round. Since Einstein said $E=mc^2$ we have been catapulted into the era of more with less technology."

His head was like a child's, it seemed bigger than his body. He was like a clown on a beach, or sitting at the end

148

of a pier with a pile of bottles beside him already corked with prophecies and parables which he threw into the ocean of our energy. He was hope. After a decade of CND and no progress but the horrors of science, the threat of world destruction that hadn't happened — here was simple scientific faith, hope and charisma.

"In my father's time the average distance covered by a human being was 3,000 miles. I have covered three million. I am still alive.

"I want to ask you a question: how much does the *SS Queen Mary* weigh? How much does a Boeing airplane weigh?" He waited for no answers. "Which carries more people across the Atlantic? The Boeing by doing more with less. I was working in the Navy Department in World War One. We had to think in terms of performance per pound. Then I left the Navy and went into building. I was amazed. How many of you here tonight know what this building weighs?

"A few years ago in America, all electricity companies were privately owned, competing with one another. Then we invented the half million volt grid system. So it became possible to send large currents of electricity over great distances. And in America there is a time lapse. When New York has a peak, Los Angeles has a low. But the electricity companies, they wouldn't co-operate until we asked them to ask a computer which would bring them more profit. To stay apart or to co-operate. And the computer said — co-operate. That's what was done. Now we can send a million volt electricity current across thousands of miles and the day'll come when we have grid lines across the Baring Straits from Siberia to Alaska, because it will pay. To join half of the world in darkness with the other that is in light.

"The computer will make man obsolete as a specialist. To give man adequate purchasing power to keep industrialisation in accelerated regeneration, we will have to pay all of humanity to go back to school, where they will generate progressively higher standards of living from fewer resources. The Malthusian scientists said man would run out of minerals, and it is true — but in the United States today 65 per cent of all steel comes from scrap. The problem is a problem of design. If you melted down all the two ton automobiles, and designed a one ton automobile, twice as many people could have automobiles using no more metal. The United States has no tin. But in scrap she has more tin than in all the tin mines of Bolivia.

"Now young people of the world, they understand this — they have been born into a world where television brings the news from world around on the hour into the home. They are the first generation to think in world terms.

"Wars have been caused because one side has, and the other has not. In 1900 only 1 per cent of humanity was living as a success. Today 44 per cent of humanity. And it is possible by design and science, by increasing the performance per pound in architecture and industrial design to make life a success for 100 per cent of humanity." He talked of the bumble bee. Of the order that is in nature. Of progress from wire to wireless.

"In twenty years we may have blown ourselves to pieces, said a computer. Yet the computer says in forty years man can make a success of himself on earth. The choice is clear: Utopia or oblivion.

"If the world goes on assuming itself to be an inherently self-frustrating system then ignorant submission to the inertia of our lethally conditioned reflexes will soon push the buttons of Armageddon. We however are betting that the Earthians will wake up and win.

"Students have a sense of justice and they get exasperated. Students ask why can't politicians make a world work? But the fact is the politicians are faced with a vacuum, and you can't reform a vacuum. If we can't reform man, we can reform man's environment.

"Now architecture is a slave profession today. Architects say what colour the doorknobs are but not how much the building is to weigh. Billions of dollars are going into the space programme, making a sky house capable of sustaining man as a metabolic success anywhere in the universe. But no scientist has ever been retained to consider the scientific design of the home of man: to design ways of employing the highest scientific potential towards helping man to be a success on earth.

"So I tell students world around, we must redesign the world's resources, for we can make life a success. It is not a bad thing to have hanging over your head — success. Students of the world are thrilled to realise it is themselves they must turn to in order to make the world work. The students know they need no more licence to invent tools that will make the world work than did the Wright brothers need a licence to invent one of the most needed more with less tools, the airplane, and students know that if they invent the right tools, they will be used, given the right emergency. When you students have by your model taught the world to see the problem and the clearly designed model of its solution, the world, weary of artificially induced dilemmas, will vote for your LIVINGRY, forsaking the obsolete KILLINGRY."

At about this point Professor Bucky Fuller had been speaking non-stop from 7.30 to gone 11 and the caretaker came on to the podium and said "I want to lock this place up. You can't go on talking for ever." Bucky raised his hand as if he was about to be sworn in as President of the United States. "There is not much time," he said with his eyes now open, "we must take the design initiative now. I leave you. Go to work." There was massive applause. Standing ovation — and what happened then?

151

Plastic domes

We went to Paris, the student architects and me, with a plastic dome. Students all over the world were going to Paris with plastic domes — to take up Buckminster Fuller's challenge and prove to the world that mankind could be a success on planet earth. "Metabolic success" was Buckminster Fuller's phrase. He was going to be there himself in Paris, for the World Congress of Architects were to launch "The World Design Science Decade 1965–1975": it was a scheme to involve students world around in changing the consciousness of the human race. And Bucky was our inspiration.

The great invention of Buckminster Fuller was the geodesic dome: his practical example of doing-more-with-less technology that would save the world. It was designed to a mathematical principle, a tensigrity structure, like suspension bridges, so it could be as big or small as you wanted. Like very high buildings it had to sway a bit. Ours was made of metal struts and a plastic skin on which we were to paint the resources of the world: so many tin mines, so many scrap metal yards.

Bucky wanted students to show the world how man could live on earth as a success. He wasn't stupid: he did realise that most men believe they can only be successful by treading a lot of other people into the ground. Bucky knew he had quite a task, and needed all the students he could get to help him. He proposed five two year phases of a world retooling, to get the design right for success. His own university at Carbondale, South Illinois, had collected and computed and collated an inventory of world resources.

The task, at Paris, was told us by Bucky: he had a little tent, a conventional tent in which he sat, most evenings, like a scoutmaster, a mad inventor. "Students of the world: no world news will emanate from the official topic

— 'The education of an architect' — of this Eighth International Congress of World Architects in Paris, France. No — but the students of the world do have a story. The greatest. The world can be made to work, successfully for all, and we know how to do it. The one and only world revolution..."

Part 2

Battle for the slums

I believe

That I saw Christ dance
With Mary Magdalen
And drink a pint of ale
In Islington with Thomas Paine.

The talk concerned
On both occasions how
The poor in all their majesty.
Would reign one day upon this earth.

Paul Potts

A place of my own

We got home from Paris, in July 1965. I moved my flat. The three rented rooms by the cigarette factory had become unbearably over-run with guests and lodgers. It was impossible to work there. They kept all hours. It was life but the tension was terrific, and one of my lodgers was a ponce with three girls. Spreading his favours between them was a bag of tricks worth watching. The girls seemed to like being beaten up. I abhor violence, but it's there like a magnet. I've never used it myself but it is there — and was often a highlight of our days. You felt yourself being drawn into it, as into the calm centre of a tornado. That — violence, pop music, Alsatian dogs and alcohol. On the third occasion, Teresa and the television set went through the front window, I said to Brin, my long suffering flat-mate, we're leaving home.

One weekend the lodgers were away. We cleaned the flat, and left it spotless and crossed town in the dead of night with all our belongings in a push cart. I dropped the keys into the landlord's letterbox with a note, telling him to change the locks in his own interest and giving no forwarding address.

I was always tight for money. Always in debt. When I flitted from the flat I owed £100 in rent. When money came into the new place I spent it on a beautiful scarlet carpet. The old place had been furnished. The new place was unfurnished. In time, as happens, my old landlord found out where I was living and sued me for the rent I owed him. I went before a judge, or registrar, whose name was Abraham Flint, and he was a model of benevolent kindness. I was guilty. I said the landlord was a bastard. He said you are guilty, you owe the money — but, said Judge Flint, considering your circumstances you can pay the debt off by just a small amount each month. I never bothered, and before that summer was out the bailiffs called. More than once. And the head bailiff was a Mr Sims. One morning in he walks, and looks around the flat and said if I didn't pay in seven days he'd bring the van and have to take away — he looked around — your furniture's no good. How about a painting, said I — I've a nice one by Adrian Henri of Dougal in *The Magic Roundabout*. He kept looking, sniffing — never replied. "I don't know the value of painting," he said eventually, "I'll have the carpet."

Oh Mr Sims, and I intended to pay within the seven days, and maybe I could have done and without borrowing. I can't remember — but I was in bed when he came again: this time with two fellows in donkey jackets. "Lift up the bed. Be careful with him, we have to leave the bed. Just take the carpet," and before you could say Jack Robinson my lovely new scarlet carpet was carefully rolled and carried down the stairs and off drove the van. "Now!" said Mr Sims, sitting on the edge of the bed, "I'll tell you how you *can* get it back." I came to like Mr Sims, the bailiff. It cost me, but I got the carpet back. And taught me a lesson? Pay when you're ready, and don't be frightened of the courts.

Where I moved to was a nondescript land. Big houses, crumbling red brick, what had been Victorian merchants' mansions turned over into flats. Fallen pillars. Bells at every door, secondhand cars in the drive, uncleaned windows, curtains drawn, bare light bulbs and very wild gardens. You know the kind of territory — flatland, a transient zone. You take people as they come. Easy come, easy go. The local pub was a battleground. It was a commercial traveller's inn trying to better itself, converting into a Berni steak bar — trying to get rid of the scruffy types. There was no stable working class family pub like I'd known in the factory district I'd left: no corner shop, no close and nosy neighbours. I'm not complaining. It was a nice flat, high ceilings and on a main road, only fifteen minutes walk to town, and buses every few seconds.

Two of the student architects moved into flats nearby. We saw one another a lot after we came back from Paris, we didn't know quite what to do with Buckminster Fuller's inspiration. To make the world a metabolic success, how do you begin? — but it wasn't a religious call to arms, only a way of thinking, so we went drinking together, sometimes to town, and sometimes to a slum over the hill. This slum lay, from our flats, about five minutes walk. When you got to the top of our hill you looked down and almost fell into it, a steep valley absolutely choked with terraces and back yards, crammed with people and teeming with life and there were hundreds of shops open all hours God sends, and on a Sunday you could buy down there those things you weren't supposed to buy on Sundays, like nylons and tights, and potatoes. The shops were too far to carry home a bag of coal, but not too far for a loaf of bread, though I have carried bags of coal, 28-lb paper bags, on my shoulder over the hill, many times. There were one or two shops open late at night near us, but I didn't find them for many months. You see I'd known this slum before. I was already attracted to this rough district like a moth to an electric light.

When I first came to Nottingham I walked aimlessly round the streets in the centre of town: big shops and offices and warehouses, and a little off centre was the wholesale market, and the central market, and the Petticoat-Lane-like market, the cold stores and the fruit and veg market, and where the barrow boys loaded their barrows, and it was alive, alive oh, night and day, so I got to know it well. Only in the afternoon and early evening was it still. Overshadowing this markets' district was a tremendous Salvation Army citadel, and great tenement lodging houses, and towering hostels for single homeless men, and behind them a little Woodpecker Cider park where the men would sleep in the summer sun before shuffling themselves into a queue for the Sally Bash. The park must have been a graveyard because leaning on the

159

walls round the edge were upstanding gravestones, and in the middle was one solitary tomb to a nineteenth-century champion boxer called "Bendigo". There was a sculptured lion on a pedestal, and the inscription had this motto, "Out of the lion comes sweetness", just like my mum's tin of Tate and Lyle golden syrup.

And then beyond this macabre, dirty, busy market and hostel district, as if directly on the other side of the wall of markets from town, was St Anns Well Road, an absolute maze of back streets that seemed to go on for ever. I had never seen so many. Whichever way you looked, up and down the hillsides, as far as any road ahead stretched, were the tight-packed roofs of poor people's housing: and it was full of surprise. The smell of wood from a theatrical carpenter's yard up a quiet cul-de-sac. The almost Americanised good-looking, middle-aged women singing to *Music While You Work* at the brightly coloured bobbins and spindles in this undergarment factory you could look right down onto from a street on a cliff buff above. There were Greek cafés, an Italian pastry shop, shops with German sausages — strings of black sausages in the window — beautiful pastry. Polish bread with poppy and caraway seeds and a shop with nothing in the window but a globe atlas on a white slab of marble and a little old lady, like a dwarf, behind a wooden counter. The wood was curved where people's hands and money had passed, from whatever they had traded in. There was no sign outside. When you opened the door an old bell rang. You said to the lady, she always wore a top coat with fur trims, "Are you selling anything?" and she'd reply, "I might, what did you want?" Whatever you replied she'd say, "I'm afraid we're out of that."

It was a maze: amazing little houses in little narrow streets, some quiet, some steaming with people, bawling, bag-eyed, hair-matted mothers crossly pushing prams on jostling pavements; hooting traffic; old men pushing carts of belongings in the middle of the road talking to themselves. There were the big outfitters — hatters and hosiers.

There was a big pawn shop, with three brass balls outside. I took my typewriter there. Old Ando, the pawnbroker said one morning: "You're sure it is a typewriter? I had a bloke, an accordionist once. He played outside the theatre, to amuse the queues on Friday and Saturdays. On Monday, or Tuesday, he'd bring his accordion in. Take it out at the end of the week when he got his National Assistance, but one Friday he didn't come for it — and I saw him Saturday playing the accordion. Well, I rushed back to the shop and opened up and lo and behold inside the accordion case was a brick. Open your typewriter case, or shall I trust you?" Gimme more I said. No, he shook his head behind his iron bars, all those racks of junk and jewels behind him. He never gave you any more.

There was a pork pie works up one back street. White coated workers, blood bespattered, clattered metal trolleys over the cobbles, with trays of pork pies, oozing jelly, steaming hot from one makeshift outbuilding to another. They had a shop on the front street and there was a queue of smart suburban ladies outside that shop from morning to noon. They were the most delicious pork pies and by the afternoon they were sold out. They couldn't make enough. And since in redevelopment they moved to a purpose built garden factory on an industrial estate, the pies have never been so tasty as they were in those small backstreet days. There were vegetable shops, spilling mangoes and aubergines on to the pavement. Crushed oranges in the gutter and great wooden crates of common cabbage. Crates of cabbage.

There were bad streets. Clarence Street was a long, straight, dead-end street and I feared to walk down on my own. I tried it once, after the pubs had closed on a hot afternoon. It was very scary. I never did it again. I'd peep and dare and walk away in fear. Big men on chairs outside their front doors, in their singlets, brandishing their tattooed arms, sat and stared at each other across the narrow, cobbled, dead-end street. There were filthy back entries and waste crofts. At Little John Street I stumbled over a sack of dead kittens. If my dog ever went down some places, it'd get a shampoo when we got home.

For the first film I ever got involved in, with Monica Sims for the BBC, we filmed a little sequence along these streets. It was a grey day, and a cold, low cloud made the swirling coal fire smoke smart your eyes. The worst city buses seemed to run into this district. The rest of the city had six wheel trolley buses, but down these streets there were old, four wheel, hard seated, draughty things. The people got a raw deal and it made you cross, and so many streets were named after great British explorers, Stanley and Livingstone. It was a crucifixion of a life for many people.

I'd been interviewed myself on popular television by Noele Gordon and was quite a famous little fellow — but I needed some action, some great adventure. I'd rogue pals who were planning bank raids, and political friends who were any day now about to capture the Labour Party, and the students were going to redesign the world. The idea of writing a travel book was taking a long time, three years, and sounding thin and it was getting awkward answering tiresome people who said "When is this book of yours coming out in the shop? What's it about, did you say?" I needed a diversion, a war, to get into some action, and it came in 1965 in that slum, like the apple falling into Isaac Newton's lap.

Rum district

It was in a street in the heart of the worst of the district that little Pat Jordan kept his shop. Off Alfred Street Central at number 4 Dane Street, the second house of a long terraced row of three storey houses giving directly on to the pavement. Pat Jordan's front room was the shop, with tables piled shoulder high with Zane Grey and Barbara Cartland. Bookshelves and magazine racks all around the wall — books for sale or exchange, westerns, thrillers and romances. Schoolboys would always be in, pawing through the dogeared comic strips, looking for a juicy Nazi tale — not realising what went on behind the curtained door, in the back room, but knowing something did.

Now, the normal set-up of dirty backstreet bookshops, in those days, was to display in the front parlour books like *Blighty* and *The Saint* and sometimes Norman Mailer. If the proprietor thought he could trust you, he'd sidle up to you and nudge, wink, wink, make a suggestion you might like to browse through his private stock in the back where you'd find volumes of *Health and Efficiency* and some naturist magazines, and maybe something in English from the Olympia Press in Paris. Pat Jordan's shop looked like that.

People would pass through, knock, enter, and come out again. I couldn't get in at first — it seemed the prerogative of old-looking, middle-aged men in dirty raincoats with thick glasses and bald heads, or else they were young men with pimples and an intent bearing. The place fascinated me. I thought it might be a backstreet brothel for the handicapped. Every time the door opened there was a whirr of machinery and noise and I imagined lashings of porn — I was quite wrong. Knock knock... Twice at the back and when you were a trustee you'd be let in to the complete works of Marx, Lenin, Engels, Trotsky and Fidel Castro.

There was a duplicator, a telephone and piles — from the floor taller than a policeman — of international socialism kept like it was hard pornography, kept half wrapped in polythene sheets; kept in the back, away and hidden from the ordinary punters.

Jordan's International Book Store, for all your socialist literature (by post) was headquarters of a really hardcore, active, left wing pressure group of some importance in the trade union movement. Where is little Pat who kept that shop? Where has he gone? I saw him only once after we were all demolished. He was exposed in the *News of the World*. His mug shot on the front page — the brains behind the Vietnamese demonstration that stormed the American Embassy in Grosvenor Square — our Pat and that upper class Pakistani, Tariq Ali. It said "Evil Men Perverting Britain". Oh no, I thought, not Pat. He always wore a raincoat but Pat wasn't like that at all. It was an outrageous anti-socialist story smeared on the front of the *News of the World*. Our Pat. He might have enjoyed it.

But what a contempt, I thought — to hide your beliefs in socialism as if they were a sexual fetish. Why hide your fetish? But to hide your Marx and Trotsky beneath Agatha Christie. These people had nothing to do with the area. They said with a grand gesture: these streets round here are symptomatic of the capitalist disease. When capitalism is overthrown, the area will be rebuilt in the interests of the working class. In the meantime they'll do nothing to ameliorate. Did they keep their windows clean? They wouldn't do much to stir things up in the streets. Or enjoy themselves at the local pub. This was 1964–1965 and they would not propagate their message from their own front window. This cell of political dynamite lay hidden in the back room of a shop locals knew only as a smutty second-hand bookshop. An elite of vetted outsiders, they stepped into the back room, with its picture of Lenin, duplicator, telephone, and first class library of political books and journals. But at that time everyone seemed engaged in secret operations.

There was another entrance, another "gate" to the district I used at night. I'd often come here from town for a different kind of drinking. There was a footbridge leading from the YMCA, high above the railway tracks. It was a public right of way above the smoky station platforms: a dimly lit, lurker's passage but I found it safe; a pretty, romantic looking, wrought iron pedestrian bridge. In fact it looked really scruffy and scrap irony in the daylight, but at night with the smoke from the steam trains and your footsteps echoing as you walked across, it was romantic: like walking into an Alfred Hitchcock film, or one of those sulky commercials for Strand cigarettes: "You're never alone with a Strand." You'd hear the train announcements: the old Gresley engines hooting with the Master Cutler at 9.05. You felt like you were crossing into another world, on the wrong side of the tracks; a world you had to respect, that had its own laws; badlands as warm as a womb where the greatest crime is thinking you know it. The first pub you came to was a little backroom bar the size of a parlour, full of lesbians, a piano, and packed. I loved it. The streets were crowded with life at night, poor and low life: more apron-tied mothers, bawling out at their child among a squad of squawking kids, scruffy and arrogant as street commandos. They didn't need adventure playgrounds in those days: the whole district was a combat zone, a battlefield.

There were scores of parlour-sized public houses, each a stone's throw, no more than a skittle cheese, from the next, and each a vanity box of characters. If it was a crucifixion, sometimes it was an orgy. Reckless pub life. It was never boring. You'd reel from one rowdy pub into another, and feel a pin drop in the silence like a douche of cold water. There would be men with waistcoat and silver sleeve suspenders playing snooker. You could sit in the passage at the Scots Greys on a cane chair by an aspidistra in a green pot: fights would pass you by and no-one upset the aspidistra. Beautiful bar passages. Outside, ladies with jugs of frothing beer walked up steep

165

streets in carpet slippers. Broody sullen pubs. No-one cared, it seemed, and everyone was up to something. People came up to you in the street and said, "Would you like a rabbit or a hare?" or "'ave a look at this cheese wot I got in my basket." Sweaty, smelly Stilton cheese, I have never tasted better. Like the pork pies, there was good living in those slum days, if you knew where. Anytime trading.

In the King Billy there was boxing, and the pub wasn't as big as the Cabinet room at number 10 Downing Street. At the Napier there was a Spanish boy, Carlos, who played the piano, in a back room, while transvestites danced on the tables. And when camp little Albert Brown came in, a cheer went up. Famous, before the war, in a morals case. He'd been done on that strangest of all British crimes that has survived all the reforms of the 1960s and 70s: the charge of importuning a provocative policeman in a gentlemen's convenience. Albert was told he'd be let off if he spilled the beans about the private lives of him and him and him. And Albert kept his lip buttoned. He was beaten, so they say. He did his time, and came back to cheers, what'll you have Albert? Everybody knew Albert Brown, with his bright blond hair, our Quentin Crisp.

And when fifteen years later, I'd become chairman of the Residents' Association and all the old back streets were pulled down and a new spacious airy world was built, I invited Albert to an afternoon tea. Hired the Methodist Hall, and gave an "Afternoon Tea with Nostalgia" for all the old folks. Battleaxe Dorothy came, and the kind Vicar, and the revered old Headmistress OBE, and the lovely lady councillor who went to nick for fiddling the vote: all were there on the stage, and there was buns and songs and stories, and suddenly I spotted Albert Brown creeping in at the back door, very old, very feeble, but his hair still dyed blonde. I raised my hands. "Ssh... Albert," everyone cried. And the pianist came up to me and whispered in my ear, "If you have that thing on the stage. I'm not going to play any more. You know who it is."

"I know who it is, and you'll play, like Carlos played."

"It's Albert Brown," who kept his fucking lips shut, who buttoned his lip, who dared to be himself.

The world has changed, utterly.

The Union was the pub where I first had barley wine, a new drink, sugary and strong and lots and lots of pills to make time speed, and sold by mods from old silver snuff tins. Hashish in silver paper: learning to soften it with a match flame and a pin. It was from the Union, Joy went to Madras. She was the first hippy we knew — from such a posh home, her mother rode horses. She spent all her time in the Union until she went East. And now it's gone, demolished. Today only the lesbian bar is left — the only back bar that survived.

And all the churches have gone — except the Anglo-Catholics with their frilly religion, but they're on their own now, isolated, surrounded by the rosebay willow herb of the 1970s. The earthed-up embankments that stopped the gipsy tinkers parking. Oh there used to be so much. An old mosque in a warehouse. It's not the same. There used to be a Russian Orthodox and Greek Orthodox Church and Black congregations in tin huts with bright hats wailing on Sunday afternoons. Now there's only Anglo-Catholics and the little ladies in leather to give any colour. All the new pubs are very boring. The lesbians are isolated beneath a monster tower of flats.

The parlour pub the authorities forgot to pull down. Nobody goes in today but those who know. I hadn't been in for about two years and I went in: "I'll have a pint." Lady behind the bar says: you know what pub this is. I said, ay me duck, I do. She said: that's all right then. But then it was everywhere — pubs, coffee bars, parties, and you could prolong the night until the wee small hours when the first wholesale market café opened at half past four. Great mugs of tea.

The slums have gone. The coffee stalls. The twenty-four-hour street. I helped to pull them down — what once I loved. When I was young I had it. Every kind of life dippable into by just walking off the street, and we were an elite, the Bohemians, who had taken as a right the freedom to their own land, members of a society built on hedonism — no. No. No. Not at all like it is today. We were bent on discovery of human nature — now it's all been discovered and done in any number of documentaries you can watch on television. The magic lost. Because then it was on the streets, and street life an uncharted jungle. Up a back street, down a dark terrace, there's an opening in a cul-de-sac wall. Cross a scullery yard. Knock, knock. A door opens — a crack on a chain. A blast of hot air as from a steam engine, clouds as from mother's washing Monday and there's a Miss Josie: a black, shiny and smiling face. Miss Josie would say: "You come to the party?" I come for the party. I come for the chicken and rice. Oh she'd laugh, Miss Josie. The food, the joints, and the black jumping music that was Mr Aston's shebeen. This rum district was an after hours jungle, a thicket of shebeens and slumming queens.

First you went into the kitchen where vats of rice and beans frothed upon a stove, and in the oven were the most delicious, crunchy, tasty pieces of chicken I'd ever tasted. Tabasco sauce and something else. I wish I'd asked Miss Josie for the recipe. I so remember the taste; tongue touching palate with pleasure. There was a passageway where Mr Aston himself would stand beside a stack of cardboard boxes containing cans of Long Life beer. If the chicken 'n' beans was cheap, the beer cans of Long Life were exorbitantly expensive. You were paying for the risk. And then there was the cellar: in the cellar was music and you didn't dance. You just stood in a silent line around the damp walls... mmnn... unsmiling: being cool; smoking grass to the music which thumped. It was the first place I ever saw speakers physically move like a beating heart. I liked the noise: then. Reggae was rare, and Blacks were special. A third of the excitement of Mr Aston's Manning Street shebeen was the music: black music. *Raas* man. Rastafarian — at that time the Emperor Haile Selassie of Ethiopia was coming to Jamaica to take his children home, back to the promised African paradise, any day. Man. Then: "It's a raid!" and we scrambled out of the cellar, through the coal-hole, into the trees, trying to escape.

Dog housing

The area when it had been built was fine and dandy. In the beginning there were fields on steep slopes owned by all kinds of people. It was built up, bit by bit, by jobbing builders on the steep slopes of mostly smallholding and allotment fields in Victorian times: factories, shops and houses cheek by jowl: lots and lots of red brick, two up two down, three up three down, terraced homes for operatives and artisans. Built to let, each with a tin bath on a hook on the outside wall of the tiny lean-to sculleries. Across a blue paved brickyard an outside lavatory leant, wonky on the back entry wall, beside the dustbin, one person big — the thunderbox. Some yards were communal, some privies shared. Some had a private pocket handkerchief sized strip of garden. And at the front, a few still had iron railings.

The reign of Edward VII, old folk who surely can't really remember would forever tell me when I first stalked the district, was the golden age of standards and of pleasure: forever they harked back to lamplights and penny trams and the street cry of the midden wagon — before running water when men wore collar and stud. There were steps to donkeystone, and knockeruppers' poles tapped on your window for alarm clocks, and coppers spanked wayward children on the spot. There was decency and order and the regulated family pleasure of the seasons: Easter Bonnet parade, June rose show, and in September fruit and vegetable exhibitions in public house backyards: the harvest festival. Not that people grew much in their gardens.

The Labour Party made a May Day parade. In my time it was led by Ken Coates through the city and through Peas Hill Road in St Anns. Ken said it always struck him as he marched the canyon streets down there, there wasn't a blade of grass, not a touch of green to be seen.

True. Sociologists said the same: not a leaf on the drab streets of this festering slum. But when they said that publicly, later on, it hurt people because the pride of the district was an adjacent hillside you couldn't always see from the streets.

On this hillside, above the slum, were 150 acres of horticultural endeavour in which almost every family, of whatever means, took part: the allotments. Hunger Hill Gardens they were called, green and glinting with glass and so fruitful. Every pub and chapel in season displayed the vegetables from the Hunger Hills. Not so large now. We fought to keep it all but some was lost to the new houses though the gardening tradition remains, fruit, flowers and veg. sold and swapped among families or given to friends.

All houses when built are generally considered an improvement. By someone. That's the idea. And many people came to our district in the very beginning from blind back-to-backs, of medieval poverty in an overhanging district called Narrow Marsh. Almost everyone agreed, what is now the slum, was an improvement on that. In the nineteenth century people eagerly put their name down with the builder or agent to rent one of these improved dwellings built entirely by private enterprise on streets named to honour the glory of Empire: Calcutta, Curzon and Bombay. Only a very few bought their own. The builder's relations did — they would live in the corner house faced with slightly better brick and a little larger. A few villas and shops were later built. Some public houses were substantial and some factories very big: clothing and engineering, printing and those pork pies. There were chapels and, running through the middle of the district, a very grand, tree lined avenue — by Aston's shebeen. These were originally grander houses — a Victorian promenade, closed to motor traffic: a bracelet of green maturity, adding a real touch of class now as it did then. It was not demolished. No-one suggested it should be. We fought to extend it but the compromise we won was a very

171

nondescript New-Townish pedestrian path lined with vandal-torn flowering cherry.

The first houses to be condemned were in George V's reign, after sixty years of life, marked by public health authorities as unfit for human habitation. They didn't get pulled down. They didn't get improved — except earth closets were replaced: and the sound went of the ten o'clock horses — as the carts were called that changed the night soil. Though parents would still cry to their children, "If you don't get to bed the ten o'clock horses'll get you." Good riddance to that cry of the past. The smell must have been abominable.

In the Depression some men were unemployed but most kept in some kind of work, on low wages — traditionally people were paid low wages — working in the markets or making up textile smalls, hose, blouse, stockings, in little sweatshops, mostly, with much piecework and plenty of outwork for the old and pregnant and disabled, for women as well as men worked. And that is still the pattern.

Rents were low and though there were many landlords and they changed, but rarely did a landlord sell to a sitting tenant, and even more rarely sell freehold. By George VI's reign a prudent few had saved a deposit and bought themselves, with a mortgage, a house of their own — and it had to be in the suburbs. The old district was not what it was. And it was difficult to buy a house in St Anns. Families who were overcrowding put themselves on the council housing list and if the overcrowding was proven enough, enough times, they were moved from a tight terrace to a garden suburb council house. The council had built lots of garden suburbs in the 1920s and 30s. To many people they must have seemed a paradise on earth, a real dream of escape from the crucifixions and the orgies of the back streets. And they were physically the best houses the council were ever to build. The Germans bombed the odd factory, and a few stray bombs fell on houses. Blitzed sites were cleared, on which the

172

first council houses were built in the district itself in the 1940s. Just a few.

For the rest, people seemed happy and lots of people look back to the 1940s and 1950s as another golden time for honest to goodness neighbourly folk, in and out of one another's houses, mucking in together, chasing repairs which were never done. Sons and daughters moved. Putting your name on the council list had replaced having a word with the agent. Family connections were breaking... And into the vacant *lebensraum* came Queen Elizabeth's chickens: the immigrants, like so many crowbars thrust into the crumbling cracks of our rotten brickwork. Queen Elizabeth might look young, heir to the Elizabethan age of plenty for the multitude. But in our district, we weren't in the Elizabethan age. These streets were built on the sewers of Queen Victoria. Hers was the mother country the immigrants came to in 1954–1956 — from the Commonwealth. Our old streets, their new world.

Refugees also came from Poland, the Ukraine, from Hungary. Workers — we got many poor Italians seeking work here in the 1950s and they settled and stayed, for some reason. And the Irish and the Scots, and all the casual, poor white British Islanders, from broken homes and broken lives, uprooted and lodging in our district to build new motorways and the great power stations on the River Trent. So they had plenty of money, sending some home from our post office, and spent the rest in public houses. They lived in shabby rooms in shabby streets. And when their contract finished they were caught in a dilemma. To go home, or to stay and get their tax back and the social security, claiming off the Welfare State. They couldn't do an odd job for you, because the Social'd cut you off if they found out. And on the edges of the area, students began to settle where the gas lamps shone brighter, on streets with occasional trees, where the housing fabric was not so mouldy and the landlords had cared enough to make down a villa into flats.

173

But in the heart of the district, in the valley bottom, where the smog from smoking chimneys hung, where on damp days houses leaked and sweated with drip, and on hot days walls flaked, in closed terraces off narrow streets, landlords' agents had forgotten who the landlords were: agents of agents of principals too weary to care a damn for too long a list of troubles. The bad drains were constant. Brick walls collapsed all the time. In a gale I'd shelter from the falling slates. Accidents. Incidents. Lead nicked. The few iron railings Beaverbrook forgot to take for the war effort vandals tore out of stones to hurl as spears.

Far away, when the lists were eventually published of individual landlords they read like the coach station at a Bank Holiday. Many had addresses at the seaside. And the institutions who still owned houses owned them only in name — they could make money out of the new capitalism: unit trusts, you've never had it so good. By the 1960s a gentleman of property meant the corporate owner of an office block. Only the stupid and the old owned poor people's houses — and the loyal poor and the peculiar and the crooked like Rachman.

The local railway station on a minor inner city loopline closed in 1920. Trams were replaced with trolley buses and the streets throttled with growing motor traffic. Some backyard firms had expanded greatly. There were questions in the House of Commons about Pork Farms pork pies pounding, pumping and steaming through a nightshift while neighbours up the yard tried to sleep in tiny bedrooms on sweating summer nights. Other firms contracted — leaving dangerous, derelict dens. Children were killed, and when that or a serious accident happened, then gangs of cross mums would gather at street ends to stew their impotent old rage. It made you sick — this place, them, society, this district.

In 1958 the summer was very hot and there was a race riot of national significance at the bottom of the tree-lined avenue, the Robin Hood's Chase. It lasted several nights and preceded the race riots at Notting Hill in London. The history of our race riot has never been researched and written up, and it would be interesting. My co-chairman on the Residents' Association for some years, Mick Waplington, who was a local Ted on the streets at the time, fiercely maintains it was a domestic brawl the television news latched on to, and when television brought their arc lights and ex-army trucks into the area to film the street at night, people came from all over to get a good butcher's, to gawp and gape. And then the trouble started. There was more trouble because of television than race.

The publicity provoked a gusher of official people, uptown, asking questions and coming down to take a proper dekko. And everybody of any responsibility thought something must be done about that district. They gasped when they looked, it was a problem — like Topsy — it had grown out of all proportion. It really was in a shocking state. By 1965 things were very bad. It was impossible to pinpoint the blame and clearly no one individual, no one authority, could attempt to tackle it. It needed comprehensive treatment. So officials wrote reports of recommendations and passed them from one to another. Public Health continued to list, as they had since the 1930s house after house unfit for human habitation. It reminded me of one of my dafter childhood collecting manias. When I was about seven, I'd go along streets writing down door numbers in a little red notebook. 2. 4. 6. 8. 10. 12., and you might get an 11a. 11. 9. 7. 5. 3. 1. Pages of them. Every house identical. Every house condemned: terrace after terrace. There were few exceptions. The inspector never had a good word. Conditions were terrible, and these sewers were used, these condemned houses were lived in. Here begins the story of failure.

Battlefields

City officials had been looking at this district for some time, but the new City Architect was looking harder, and with an architect's imagination, and an artist's determination. One of the students got a vacation job, when he came back from Paris, working as an assistant in his office. He came across the first imaginative sketch for tearing everything down in St Anns, and filling the valley with Le-Corbusier-like modern architecture. Imaginative, future age stuff, from hillside to hillside. He was flabbergasted.

In the art gallery I organised a Saturday civic talk-in and invited and got almost every new brain in town. The talk, morning and afternoon, before and after little drinkies, was not of Buckminster Fuller and how to save planet earth, but our city: the place we lived in. Little speech after speech, sensible debate and interruption, proved town planning as the number one issue of the moment, and what to do with that slum was on everybody's tongue. A regional architecture, glossy monthly magazine had just begun, and the young editor was a dynamic person, very keen — how else do you describe them? Smart dressers with pushy ideas. Here was a great chance, he said, fallen by providence on our generation, and it should not be botched. He moved away later, and did very well designing North Sea oil things, and gas installations. Very well. But then we were going to rebuild: we were so keen on our town.

The man who redesigned Coventry, from the ashes after the Blitz, was now living among us, a Professor at the University. We were impressed. The County Architect was a *bon viveur*. We went to his place for parties. He was pioneering a method of more with less technology that could build good new schools cheaply. There was an art teacher, Paul Ritter, who had a Wilhelm Reich orgone box.

He was an influence: he later went on to plan the new city of Perth, Western Australia. Live wires. Sparks of the future — we could almost touch it.

On the streets it was very different. There was nothing of the future but rottenness, and no promise, but the whisper of rumour was rife. Hopelessness was gaining ground. The students had to prepare a thesis for their final year and three of them asked if they could combine and write a joint thesis — a rare request: studying together the redevelopment prospects for St Anns. They'd jumped in a month from the thoughts of world mankind as a metabolic success to our own backyard. The slum would be handy for where they lived. It was *the* talking point of town: everyone had an opinion, and it was the city authority's mammoth task ahead. It had to be got to grips with. The college teachers said yes, but be careful. Down there is a political minefield. Professional people must practise discretion.

The students went out, and in the name of "the thesis", they interviewed officials and experts. Everyone talked to them. It was as if the boffins and bureaucrats welcomed talking, freely and fully to students, in confidence, for a thesis: it must have been a kind of release from keeping their mouths shut. For their plans were being prepared as if the public were an enemy. And not only were the city officials not telling the public anything, they weren't telling each other very much. It was a big area (340 acres). So little had been done in the past, maybe they felt guilty: the size of the problem was frightening. It was one of the largest backstreet districts left in Britain — 30,000 people.

Every department saw themselves with a unique chance to fulfill their dreams. A perfect world. Plans were concocted in deadly earnest, and in dead secrecy: laid uptown by different council departments, in a conspiracy, like a plot against the realm. For fear of alarming the people was a reason they gave. They wanted to wave their plans in the air at the auspicious moment. For the pride of the department.

177

Each department jealously guarded its schemes from every other department's prying eyes and ears. Education were not telling all and sundry what they were planning, until the ripe time: the right time. The fire brigade were certain they were going to build the perfect fire station: they'd a deal for a site absolutely promised, cast iron. The architects were equally certain they hadn't. Nobody told Social Services anything, so owning nothing and being new they could make no concrete plans. The City Engineers, being the road builders, assumed everyone would have — Hobson's choice — to fit in between the blank spaces in their concrete highways plan. The architects, equally certain the housing pattern would come first, should come first and everything fit around that. The planners could see both sides' points of view, but there were outside considerations, they said. The national motorway pattern. The government was involved. They'd have to finance all these capital schemes, or give permission for the council to borrow the money needed. It would be millions.

The Town Clerk was a new man, appointed as the wizard to roll together the dreams of his bureaucrats into a computered programme. He did — eventually: and much faster and more successful than anyone dreamt possible. But the council were only part of the picture then. The future was to be all theirs — but then there were other forces. The brewers had fifty-seven public houses. There were freeholders of land, who might part without a fight, if the council offered them land elsewhere, like an industrial estate. There were factory owners. There were the churches. The churches were amazing: they pondered in secrecy the disposal of their properties, land and church buildings without ever telling the incumbents. The vicar was kept in the dark. Secrecy and intrigue were everywhere. Poor ward politicians tried as best they could to understand what was going on, but the middle-grade officers who were actually drawing out the plans were not allowed to tell them, so the politicians put together their own platform of platitudes. Something they thought would win them votes.

We talked among ourselves. I introduced the students to Ken Coates. He was at it too. He'd teamed up now, with Billy, my old election agent, in the Vote for a Madman campaign. The two of them were running evening classes at the Workers' Education Centre about the sociology of the poor: poverty, deprivation and morale. They took their class down there, asking questions and getting harrowing tales. Doing a survey. They said to us: when we reveal what's coming out in our interviews, if our hunches are proved, and when we release this news — if it is as it's shaping up — then it will blow this town sky high. The poverty is desperate, and statistically provable. The low wages. The number of people without a bathroom. If they are rehoused as they ought to be, how are they going to pay new high rents?

We talked to Cordley. He was still around: he'd done a film down there: he called it *Dog Housing*. Burn it down, said Cordley, and shoot the rich and council lackeys.

In a grand house that lay between my rooms at Rotting Villas and the students' flats there lived a real fine woman: one of the best of those busybody, world-interested, liberal minded women. She was the wife of the professor in charge of Ken Coates: mother and housewife and with time to make coffee for me in the mornings and let me use their telephone. She was a gossip. I mean that nicely. She knew the students: they were very bright, she said. She knew the slum. Like us, she shopped there too, sometimes. She knew all kinds of different people. She said you must do something, with all this material and interest you're building up.

Certainly I was enjoying myself, delving and stirring and eager to have a new theme in my life: something to do that would be real, and engage me and have meaning and that I could do. I mean, book reviewing and broadcasting and drinking and painting street objects a puce colour and writing "Nothing is forbidden" outside lavatory walls was not enough to occupy my mind. So there I was still young, a late youth, full of fit beliefs in a future we could capture, in rebelliousness, and I'd had enough pleasure in life: I wanted more and other, deeper things. There was purpose now when we went pub crawling in the slum. And so the drift began into radical community politics. There was no-one else we could copy in the city, and few in the country. In the beginning it was just me and the three students. They said we're coming up with this alarming array of semi-secret information we just can't keep to ourselves. It must be passed to the people, but we are apprentice architects and dare not reveal it in our name, for the sake of our future careers and passing examinations and wearing that degree is important to us and our families and our future families and professional discretion is a code, an ethic we won't break.

The students said you have got to help us: we will be the ears, you be the mouth. Did they? — or was it me forcing myself on them, saying let me take the information you've picked up and I'll blow the gaff? What right had I? None: self-appointed. Beholden to no-one, immersed in the middle of the incredible 1960s with my Bohemian background, an ageing youth. With this romantic belief in "the people" and "struggle" and "revolution", and this slum for my stamping ground. Tone down your floweryness, said the apprentice architects, and voice our simple sense, tell the people plainly what we see.

We all agreed that we found the secrecy appalling. As piece by piece, like detectives, we whittled the truths, there were too many, too conflicting: we didn't trust them. Even more surprising, there was no leadership on the streets. No Workers' Revolutionary Party. No National Front in those days. No People's Rights; no tenants' association. We'd have to form one. The churches were moribund. There was no campaigning vicar. One cleric always on the streets up-town demonstrating against the oppression of blacks in South Africa, but about their own district, they did the best. They were very worried about their own future. There was no radical writer like Alan Sillitoe who came from our district, no *agent provocateur* we could use to speak what people were frightened of saying.

The political parties were conservative, no maverick councillor in that district, at that time — they were all asleep or waiting for the Apocalypse. The Liberal Party did not exist. The ward Labour Party was extremely weak, and the Conservative Party stronger in both organisation, activist support from shopkeepers, bunfights, beanos, and sometimes even popular votes. Ken Coates was very interested, writing his report. Pat Jordan's International Socialist bookstore was to set the world on fire. There was no grassroots leadership in the area, for the area — and yet there was life on the streets with a capital L. People helped one another. There was real cameraderie, but no organisation. No Women's Institute. No lord of the manor. No parish council. No caped crusader. And the landlords didn't care, and the council was in a conspiracy of silence.

There was a tremendous fight ahead and the people must be armed. But not only would we have to supply the ammunition, we'd have to create the army, from scratch. We searched the correspondence columns of the evening papers. There were no "good" letters. We eyed the pubs, the shops for talent — there was no natural focus for leadership. We would have to break the people out.

It was necessary. For example, the Public Health had been listing all properties, finding out exactly who the true owners were and these lists were kept secret.

Another example: the one city department that was making moves was for road building. How I under-estimated in the early days the council official who was in charge of buying property. He was a strategist, with a real sense of timing and an almost military force. It was not proposed to build the motorways until the 1980s, but this canny man realised with land values declining in the slum, against the normal upward trend, he could get future urban expressways built through our district with little opposition. And he'd begun buying land, on behalf of his council, fifteen years in advance of its use, with or without houses, whenever the price was right.

He was a real general in charge of a long war. He was a master spy playing chess. He was buying when the going was cheap and he was buying tactically — letting this one odd buy depress a neighbourhood, lower the value of a street, so whoever and whenever in the council decided what eventually they wanted to do, he would be able to offer them the land on which to do it, as cheaply as possible, to the advantage of the general ratepayers of the city. The line proposed for the road was his priority, and he enjoyed the game of it all. He was a really dangerous man.

Many people were going to their landlord's agent, pleading for vital repairs to drains and roofs. They had no joy. Sometimes we discovered the houses were not owned by the private landlord any more. He thought he'd sold them to the council — but his name stays on the rent book. Our wily man had started negotiations. He'd say to the old landlord, you administer it for a bit: take the stick. A wise move. Because if the tenants could prove the council had become their landlord they could be shamed into doing those repairs. It suited the council to keep the old landlord's name on the books. Negotiations do take time: this purchase has not finally been completed. Your landlord is in limbo and there's a hole in your roof. Deliberately our district was being run down by the civic protectors, the electors, the city council. I don't mean the council had decided that. They hadn't. They'd have been, and they were shocked when they found out about such "dirty tricks" — but so it goes. It was a war. It was money. That was why the officials were keeping quiet. But what this practice of "civic violence" did was snuff the spirit in gentle people. Those who had tried to make good homes felt it wasn't worthwhile, carrying on. They were losing the stomach to protect their little palaces: their hearts were not in it as systematically, day by day, the area got worse.

It was a common dirty tale. We knew it was happening, and we knew who was doing it: coldly and callously public officials, for the sake of the greater good, were letting a way of life die. Of course the people didn't know the facts, but they sensed it. They knew their streets weren't getting tender loving care. And when authority sets such morals... when they let an area run itself down good and bad, decline by not sweeping the streets or quickly cleaning the drains, letting derelict houses lie derelict and the paint peel on every public facility but the black painted lamp-posts, such a lack of tender loving care from the council, makes it very difficult for individuals who want to improve themselves. Get out — or give up.

The leaflet

Time was short if we wanted to influence real decisions. To get people to come out I needed an organisation, and there was none so we invented this Tenants' and Residents' Association. I'd read in *Freedom* of a man who called himself a residents' association and had great effect, though there was only the one man and his dog. We would print a leaflet, a handbill, and by law in Britain such a thing must carry an address of the perpetrator. We used my name and address, and the wife of one of the students. We had it printed super duper professionally, a big leaflet, a long thing with a huge question mark on the front of the foldout — Whither St Anns?

We said the council's eventual intention of knocking the whole district down, when they get round to it, must be challenged — when will they get round to yours? By what date? In what order will the streets be felled? They just can't blow them all up, homes for 30,000 people with one bomb drop. It'll take years. How many years before they reach your place?

And we distributed the leaflets all over, all around the edges of the area to let the fringes know of the panic there must be in the valley slum below: so people in no (apparent) danger would sense the trouble afoot and check themselves out. Where did this motorway go? We printed all the secrets we'd garnered from authorities. We said an end to the secrecy: let's have it all out in the open. We printed our general knowledge of demolition, its consequences and the alternatives.

We questioned the council's ability to build a new better world. Was there the money to build a new town within a city? This was at the time Shelter, the national campaign for the homeless, had been going for about a month, and reckoned there were a million people without a home in Britain. A home or a proper home, I never discovered — but it seemed a madness to knock good houses down. The students had been talking to people, house to house, interviewing and — although many people said they wanted the hell out and to take the new world, whatever will be will be — when they listened a little longer to people, there was an appreciation of the cheap living: they enjoyed the shops, the variety of entertainment, the nearness to Granny and to town. My romance about backstreet life had some foundation: it wasn't all Bohemian stuff and nonsense. People were as fearful, as sceptical of the new as we were: crazy new housing schemes; higher rents; leaving neighbours for overspill estates and high rise blocks.

No one was going to be given a choice: no-one was going to be asked. Unless you spoke up quick and loud, it would be too late. People are asked to bear the burdens of the present in the hope of a glorious, but unspecified future. Plans for your eventual transportation to paradise mean life now must be a hell. Toil on. It's sad for your children to play in shit. And the future planned becomes rosier the longer the wait. Of course the bright and the lucky and the fleet get out, even rats desert a sinking ship and all that will be left in our district will be the weakest.

The plans being prepared by military minds, will be shown only when it's too late for change: they are no plans in a democracy, they are a dictatorship. When revealed they will be broad and sweeping. One old lady I knew went to the Planning Office making enquiries: what happens to my house? What will replace my street? Where will I go? She came away with no satisfaction. She said to me, "I know more about the avenues of the Kingdom of Heaven, than the planners' streets." As things turned out, there were to be no streets. All the new thoroughfares would be cul-de-sacs called Close and Walk, and given neutral names. There would be nothing as straight as a street.

We knew people. The students had interviewed people, and I had talked to people in pubs who were adamant they wanted to stay in the area, didn't want to be shifted, though there were always a lot of ifs and buts. They would stay if they could move to a little larger house, or one with a garden; or stay put where they were but have an inside lavatory, a flush loo put in, poison the next-door neighbour's dog, or have a bathroom added to their existence, seriously. Couldn't that be provided? The present was dreadful because some of the best people wanted to put a bathroom in and they weren't allowed to do so, some were able with their own money, hands and time. Not many, but there were some. With grants there could have been more. They only needed planning permission, and all permissions had been kyboshed until the future was determined and revealed. No permission and so no bank, no building society would lend you money. It was illegal to improve: in that valley or anywhere near it. Everyone hedged until they found out the truth of the future. A blight was on St Anns.

Imagine the new paradise could be built. The old way of life would have to be razed to the ground: the area's history would be obliterated wholesale: generations of experience have no more continuity. The nineteenth and twentieth centuries have no more physical presence in our district than the passing through of the Vikings. We knew — big demolition, big builders, people decanted — a virgin site — new world delayed — weeds flourish. We'd seen it happen. Swatches of our inner cities in 1965 had lain fallow for years. Demolished to bring down the number of slum dwellings. They could afford to demolish. Tell a contractor and he'd take rubble away for free for motorway foundations. But can you afford to rebuild? Can you ever agree on what to rebuild? And what was a community lies wasted, desolate. You've lost a city. You've broken a heritage from generation to generation.

Another reason — even if wholesale demolition and comprehensive redevelopment worked and gave people good, cheap, decent, new homes and environment — the present conditions would linger for many people for many years, until the big demolition machine reached their sub-area. In many terraces to let, people would have to endure the present conditions for another seven years more or so, that we thought would be criminal. The accidents: the disease: the tension. The charge in the court of public history would be murder, though, for some councillors, murder with diminished responsibility. Seven years is a child growing up. The brickwork of some houses was absolutely rotten: the earth at the back of some terraces almost an open sewer. Why not take the worst first, we said, it's loopy that the best chance a family has of being rehoused and demolished is to lie in the way of a future road. A road we didn't see as necessary to criss-cross an old world or a New Jerusalem: motorways like a cross-your-heart bra. Their pie in the sky when what we want is common sense and now.

The student-architects had made progress with their study. They were quite certain it would be a dreadful waste were it all knocked down. We put it in the leaflet. It was taking a long while to write, this leaflet. "Let the worst houses be knocked down quickly, like yesterday." And then, we went on, let the not so bad, the patchable, be patched up. Let those with room to be improved, be improved, and save, retain and encourage the good. Strengthen them. For the present. Do something. No more dilly-dallying. No more shilly-shallying. No grand schemes to wave in people's faces. Let something happen now, and let the people do it. We were searching for slogans — WORST FIRST.

The students' thesis was working itself into a scheme. They'd begun talking with builders and working it into some practical detail. I know most radical students are supposed to be plainly left wing and broad-sweeping, and away with all the old ways — but it wasn't like that. They didn't, and I didn't, find it any effort to think small is beautiful: years before Schumacher published his book. Buck's domes were small. We were reading Samuel Smiles' *Thrift and Ecclesiastes* — but most of all we were using our eyes and ears. I thought the students' scheme was marvellous, and I still do. It had to be tested. The leaflet was to put it to the public.

In the leaflet we put forward the bones of the students' plan without admitting to being students. We were against the trend of knocking everything down. It sounds so easy, and is so fraught. We were against the secrecy.

I added a literary phrase of my own, remembering how my mother kept me away from the school dentist who seemed to be always extracting everything from poor children's mouths. "A good dentist," we put this in the leaflet, "is loath to pull all a man's teeth out." We called attention to particular streets, naming them — good and bad. It was surprising how many people didn't know the condition of streets that lay but two blocks away, behind the opposite side of the street where they lived: all their lives they never look about them. Oh, we thought we were very clever. Jumping up and down all over the parish, hooting from the rooftops summat's afoot. Everybody had a finger in the pie — so let us too: make the public form demands.

We wanted the leaflet to be read by the people on the streets, and the people up-town in authority and influence. We printed more than we needed and we printed in three versions. One, abbreviated, was in green. There was a leaflet of medium length in yellow, and a full version in white. Like the porridge bowls of the three bears in *Little Red Riding Hood*. The idea was, if we put different colours and different lengths of leaflet in adjacent doors, neighbours would gossip more about our message. "I've got a yellow one." "Oh I've got the green." "I've got a white." "What does yours say?" "No, mine doesn't say that: let's have a dekko at yorn."

We were wrong. We were wrong about so many things. It was the first piece of paper in anyone's letterbox about the future. Fact or question — and it was dynamite. We'd appealed on the leaflet for people to write to authority: let their landlord and the council know their opinions, and also to get in touch with us to build a people's organisation. I'd expected an avalanche of mail. That didn't happen. I was heartbroken. We'd debated and agreed, and written and paid the printer, trudged and distributed these leaflets to every home: delivered 15,000 handbills by hand ourselves over one snowy weekend in February 1967 — and the response was two. That's not quite true. I had twenty letters in three days, all from one person, all in Ukranian and all with more than the necessary stamps. They were all complaining (I had them translated) about persecution in the Ukraine. Had them translated by both rival Ukranian clubs.

I had a letter from a Mr Lofthouse. He was the first indigenous man I fell in love with in this campaign. He was a sweet man, Mr Lofthouse, a bachelor. He lived in a terrible, old, pokey house and was so happy because it was cheap. He wanted to fight, and I treated him really rotten in the end. I haven't seen him for years now. I hope he's content. He had real sensitivity.

The student's wife was approached personally by a lady who ran a baby shop. She said she might join, because it might help her get information, and she would put a poster in the window. That was something. I had a letter from a friend, a fellow journalist I didn't know lived down there. She wrote for one of the county papers. She was a charming single lady. I called for tea. She'd faced a great deal of tragedy in her life, and lived discreetly in a ground floor room of what had been a builder's house, with a nice archway and a stable at the back — disused — but it could have been an attractive mews. I told her, thanks for writing, will you organise your street, or they'll have the place down: get involved and help us winkle out more information and put the pressure on for common sense. Lobby and fight for what you want. She was very fond of her home. She said: "Why would they want to pull a nice place like this down?" Because, I said, you're inside the boundary of the area and they want to pull everything down.

189

"Oh, Ray, don't be ridiculous," she said, "this is the Woodborough Road district. The slum area is streets away — isn't it? — further down, and I agree with what you wrote — it's shocking. I'll do anything I can to help these poor people. It should have come down years ago. But up here — well, the terraces round about are little palaces and if anyone made any silly threats to pull this down, well, I'm very well connected with friends in high places, you know. People are different up here. It's the people who make slums, make them scruffy, not the property."

She never believed me. Demolition plans were eventually laid for her area and published. Meetings were held: we held them. She never came. She wouldn't attend. There were reports in the press she must have read naming her house number, but she wouldn't believe it until, eight years later, she saw the bulldozer — and she was an extremely intelligent, sophisticated lady. It was amazing, as the drama unfolded, it was really creepy how many people used it as a grand backdrop to some private drama. I think she was wanting the final tragedy of having her home taken off her, and being forcibly rehoused in a council flat she could forever curse. Normally active busy people, in charge of their lives, became paralysed and completely out of character — they did nothing until the great "it" was done to them.

The ordinary people were involved in the conspiracy of silence and underhand dealing. They were party to it. Few honest poor will ever admit to a stranger that they live in a slum. It's like naming names, pointing a finger. The consciousness of what was happening, many people pushed back into their subconscious. A lot who lived in the district would deny they did so.

15,000 leaflets distributed and only two real replies from "leadership material". A young mother wrote me. She was bringing up a large family decently in a tiny three storey house on a really shocking terrace. It was built on top of a cliff, yet in such a way they never saw

190

sunlight. The city authorities were dividing the whole area into sectors, each to be dealt with as their number came up. She was in Phase Four, but she wanted to get out now for the sake of the children's health. While they were small children they were in most danger. She didn't want to have to wait, and our slogan WORST FIRST appealed to her. They were one of the worst, and with great energy she organised a petition. Unanimously all the terrace signed it.

She worked with us with joy and gusto. She enjoyed our company. The campaign was not only right but fun. Until one day I called and her husband answered the door and put his foot down. "My woman's not coming out to play today," he said, or words similar, and when I met her at a street meeting she was very subdued. She said: "You see, me husband's Labour. He won't let me help any more. You're not to call again."

Wanting to queue jump, people had accused them. Not willing to wait their turn. We carried on battling, fiercely, but she wasn't leading the street. We cried like parrots: "worst first" — but the authorities persisted "sector by sector": for the contractors' convenience, demolition was done by numbers. It was a public display that the world had lost its reason and gone topsy turvy. Beautiful villas in the first phase were demolished, while people a few streets away, like this lady, lived in hovels: with no help it seemed but to wait until their number was reached. She was stuck there for ages. A cruel irony, their phase number was put back, from Phase 4 to Phase 6, for the ease of the bulldozers. A neighbour told me later it was hanky panky the husband suspected me of. It wasn't true.

The other real reply was from a man in the first sector who wanted his home to stay up. He joined us, and he succeeded. His response to our leaflet was the one that proved so fruitful. It was worth 15,000 to get just him. He made us a force to be reckoned with in town. Old Arthur had just retired. His house was in good condition, but in Phase One, scheduled for demolition soon. It wasn't a villa but a well-built terrace, two up two down: hot water, a bath and a fit outside lavatory, adjacent to the back door. He came up one frosty morning, on his bike, to see the student's wife. Jacki said he just stood there in his bicycle clips. A little man. Could he come in? He wasn't going to talk on the doorstep. When he was inside and the door closed he still stood. No, he wouldn't sit. He wouldn't have a tea, and he produced from his pocket our leaflet, the full version.

"Are you responsible for this?" he said serious as a chapel Sunday. "I have a few questions to ask, before I say anything, because this is important to me. First of all I want to know, is there anything political behind this leaflet?'

No, said Jacki, none of us are a member of a political party.

"Mmmnn," he said, "mmmnn — is there any money involved? I haven't very much. Been a working man all my life, and now I retire and the council threaten to take my home away. I'm going to save my home — if I can — I'm going to fight all the way. I've prepared it for myself and my wife. I want to save it because, as you say in your leaflet, it is shocking — it is wrong to knock good property down. A waste of ratepayers' money. But are you sincere — or is this some come-day-go-day student prank?'"

Oh, when Jacki told me, I remember thinking to myself: this is where the pranks stop. If I hadn't been entirely sincere when I began, if it had been just another adventure — then this man, Arthur Leatherland, made me serious when he said: "Right, I'll work with you," and shook hands, he meant it. He did. Our first indigenous man, a real local, born and bred, lived all his life in the district. A man of principle and strength. Like my father. It was to change my life.

The wish-street map

Unlike the lady who wanted to get out now, have her house destroyed and be rehoused, and so got all her street to sign a petition, when our Arthur organised his petition, he couldn't get everyone on his street to sign.

We properly typed the petition heads for both of them. I did it. Arthur's read: "We the residents of Cromer Road, Chandos Street and Ransom Road want our houses to stay up."

"Always keep your petition heads short," Arthur said when he door-knocked the petition round. He explained: "That doesn't mean you want to live here for ever yourself. Just that the houses are good and it's a waste to pull them down." But a lot wouldn't sign. There were a lot at the top of the street, owned by the council, and they were frightened of signing against the council. The rent collector would victimise us. We'd never get repairs done. We have to do what the council says. The fatalism in people was so deep.

In the middle of Arthur's street, the reason for not signing was the opposite — an ill-founded opportunism. They were owner-occupiers and some of them fancied that a deal with the council could be good if they played their cards right.

"You can't win," they told Arthur, "against the council. You've got to look after yourself — number one. You're wasting your time with this petition. We agree with you, Arthur, but if they see our name on this petition, how is that going to help us get a nice price?'

I went to see Arthur, two or three times every week, for five years, longer: every week from when we first met. He was a stern man. First meeting we sat there in his parlour. Gave each other potted biographies. I told him a lot about my father. He wasn't impressed by books. He wasn't an educated man, like that. He was rough — the *News* of *the*

World on Sundays. Black coal fire. Collar and stud. Then he said to me, the second time I called. "Would you like a walk to my allotment? Have you the time?" I would. I did, and on the Hunger Hills he became a different man. He said: "I don't like talking about these things in front of my wife. She's a good woman. She worries — all women do — and she doesn't fully understand, and I don't want to burden her."

Arthur was very troubled by the world. We would look down from the Hunger Hills on to the whole city, spread before us. In the foreground our backstreets, and then the city offices: the skyscrapers they were just beginning to sprout. It was March, a good month for the gardens. Mr Leatherland, I said. "Call me Arthur," he'd say, "when we're on the allotment, just the two of us. You don't have to call me Mr Leatherland up here." But I never felt he was an equal to me, just a pal. He was always an elder. He used to like me for calling him Mister in public. It had an edge to it, for both of us.

"I used to vote, used to belong Labour," he said, "support the Labour Party but they're not for the working man any more: do you realise that?" He spoke to me, eyeball to eyeball, softly like he was imparting some secret heard in the Freemasons' Hall. I said, maybe there are no working men any more.

"Mmmnn, I fear for this country: no-one wants to work."

Sometimes he'd say mmmnn and there be nothing said for five minutes. I'd still be with him. I'd learnt by now, the importance of being still. On the hill it was fresh. He'd pot or tie fruit to canes and I'd stand or crouch, a yard or so from him. I never helped. When I sometimes asked about gardening things, he'd stand up straight, look at me, tell me a little bit. Bend down. Do something. Mmmnn — and as soon as he politely could, return the conversation to philosophy: life, society and the meaning of the modern world.

"Mr Leatherland," I said, "can you tell me..." pause. Wait for the potting to stop. Wait till he looks up, along

194

the hedge, across the city centre haze in the distance, till he looks at me. "Why is it, Mr Leatherland, we handed out 15,000 leaflets and apart from you and that Mrs Roberts — and I'm not so sure of Mrs Roberts — that's the only real replies we've had. The only people doing petitions and trying to organise their streets. Why have we had such a poor response?"

"Because," said Arthur, "people around here won't write; won't commit themselves to paper, write letters to you about something like that. Working people are frightened of signing things." We must do another leaflet, and call a public meeting. People'll come to a meeting?

"Yes, but — who will pay for the next leaflet? Who paid for the last? Where will we hire the hall? Who will pay for that?" Arthur could be so boringly practical. I'll pay, I said. "What with?" Arthur said and went down to some bedding plants in a box. I told him no lies about myself. He knew me quickly. I think. He gave me a fiver towards that meeting. It was months later before I told him how much these things, like printing, really cost.

And so we did another handbill, adding as perpetrators — adding to the names of me and the students, Arthur and Mrs Roberts, and the baby-linen lady who put a poster in her shop window. The leaflet called people to a church hall we hired, for free. The vicar was very keen. We found we had friends in common, from my art gallery connections. The vicar was all for it. He just wanted to make sure we fronted it; that he and his parish council were kept in the background. Arthur trimmed my flowery style. This leaflet was printed on one side only, and we didn't repeat any metaphors about dentists and teeth. Black and white, it simply said, again — no secrets, tell the people, help the people: worst first and leave the good houses. Come to the meeting — your Tenants' and Residents' Association.

Just as we came off the allotment, with the words agreed and ready for the printers, there in that evening's paper was a Labour councillor, reported at some up-town meeting, sounding off about us. He'd produced our first leaflet and, waving it in the air, castigated us as young trouble makers. We'd been attacked. Arthur was furious: he raged and we added another paragraph to the new leaflet, naming the councillor and quoting him. "The slime," said Arthur. "Labour Party: who do they think they are?"

We have been attacked. *You* have been attacked. *We* are *you*. We didn't use those words. We quoted the councillor's attack — but words on a leaflet aren't that important. It's the message: the tone. We could walk into a public house, now, bravely up to the bar and say to the landlord — have some of these. "What's all this then?" The Association, you say, we've been attacked. There's a big meeting called for next week. "Oh," says the landlord, "I didn't know there was —" You want to come. It's going to be hot stuff, you say. See you. There's nothing like being attacked. Advertising yourself — as attacked by.

I'd been fronting general agitation for the students, and we'd begun feeding letters to the local paper. We were trying to open the subject up and the students were convinced if only we could find someone like Arthur on every street, then the idea of demolishing everything wholesale by numbers wouldn't have a chance. We needed someone on every terrace to take a petition round: to be a street leader, a street convener. The students had already been asking people door to door what they wished would happen with their streets. They were beginning to colour a map of the area showing people's wishes. To stay up, or be improved with this and that, or come down now. The big point of the meeting would be to collect more names and addresses of people willing to organise their street: be a street steward. Everyone else was doing maps, of fire stations and old sewers, condemned property and future roads: why not a map showing what people wanted — a wish-street map. Mrs Roberts wanted her terrace down now and had a petition to prove it. Arthur wanted his to stay up. We needed more: many more. A total picture of the people's desire — but 30,000 are a lot to ask.

More publicity for the meeting. We needed a news story. I put a scheme to Arthur: why not issue a public challenge to the city officials to make an on-the-spot trip down your way? You take them round your house and street yourself. Show them. Using the student-architects and my own contacts we found two high-up officials willing to say yes. Arthur challenged them, in the press. We accept the challenge, say chief officers the following day.

They met. Photo. We were news. The boffins said the houses are rather small but not too bad. Nevertheless, they must come down for the general good/the well being of the scheme/the dream of our future. Arthur was like an old steam engine at full throttle — shaking all over like an old printing press banging away, he was so furious. He'd give them what for come the meeting. We issued an invitation to councillors and boffins. It was going to be one humdinger of a meeting.

I'd been working in London that day, and the train back was late. When I came to the hall I was just in time. There was a queue in the street for the doors to open. A big queue. Very rowdy. Arthur and Mrs Roberts were inside in quite a tizz: "I didn't think you were turning up." There were plenty of students I hadn't met, come to help write down names and addresses, but they were all giggling with one another. Arthur showed me a sheaf of notes he'd prepared about his case: his street. I groaned. You won't be able to say all that, Mr Leatherland. This is a public meeting.

Some of the queue outside I knew from pub crawling were vehement down-nowers. Some councillors arrived and wriggled their way through the door, some with their ladies. They were finding chairs for one another and sitting at the front by a table at the head of the hall. "We weren't invited: you should have invited us." I said you were — councillors invited, it says so on the leaflet.

Posted one to you. "No, I mean a personal invitation: what's your name — are you this young goose?" And they laughed, like a donkey's bray: and a slap — they were the concert party come to give a turn. I said to the students, look at the councillors: we mustn't let them. Put a blackboard at the back of the hall, and be ready to pin the maps on it. Then let the people in. The people came, like a tidal wave, filling every chair, every standing space, even standing on the radiators. They made an awful noise: public hangings must have been like this.

I stood up, on a chair beside the councillors and held my arms up like we'd scored a goal, and I hollered. Those with chairs turn them round. On the blackboard at the back we'll show the plans. What they propose. What they haven't shown you. What we've half inched: from under their noses. Turn round. Jump down and whisper to a councillor's lady beside me, ever so polite: "I'll be back in a jiffy." Make way, make way, and we left them sitting on their chairs at the back with their mouths open at the insult. And I began that meeting from the back, standing on a commandeered chair. The government listened that night. I talked. The people talked. I conducted the people, grievance after grievance, not waiting for authority to reply.

Arthur spoke. I had to let him, and he went on too long, shuffling those notes, he lost his audience. He was making points by numbers. Saying, waste of ratepayers' money. He was saying, save old houses, not just my street. He was telling our message, and getting hot under the collar that people weren't paying attention. People were murmuring against him. We'd let loose a monster, a great mass moan: everyone was down now; down, down, now, now. I had to shut him up, and he looked at me like he could have cut my throat.

As the meeting closed we took names and addresses of people by the score, but I was being howled at by Arthur and councillors while others insulted. We wanted street leaders: people prepared to organise petitions and fulfil the wish-street map. But it was all confusion. Some of the student helpers didn't know the district. They didn't know the streets. They didn't know the local accent. They were writing nonsense on pieces of paper, or giving it to folks themselves to write and you couldn't read what was written. They didn't want you to read what was written. All hullabaloo broke out at the end of that meeting. The councillors said — you devious, horrible, little man. "What good are you doing? This is all a political stunt. You mark my words. The month is April. There's an election in May." I protested. They laughed — hollow laughter.

The following day I slowly walked up the Hunger Hills. I already knew Arthur well enough to be able to pick the key up from his missus and open the allotment gates on my own, remembering always to lock them behind me. It was an awkward padlock. Arthur didn't speak for a long time. "Shambles: a shambles," he said. I said I was elated. It had been a meeting of abandon and release. A great success. "Shambles," said Arthur. But the people came, 500, do you think? More? And they spoke. They opened up. We've scores of addresses to follow. We are an army.

"And my house?" said Arthur. "I'm ashamed to be associated with the shambles you organised — a rabble."

I didn't speak for a long time. Arthur, I said, why don't you write to the leaders of both political parties and the Town Clerk himself? Say to them you have been led up the garden path by us students and me, and you want a private meeting to properly make the case for your house being saved. Write to them at their homes. I'll get you their addresses. It might work.

He looked up at me, and straightened his old gardening hat. There was much feeling in his eyes. Was he crosser than ever now? Oh, what had I done? Was he going to cry?

"You think I'm like that," he looked right through me. "I won't disown you. I've been proud to meet you and Dave and Bob and the other one. If it wasn't for you I'd

199

not have had the courage to go so far with this fight. I'm in this now, win or lose my home. I'll carry on the fight, with you, together. It was a shambles, wasn't it?" All right, but the people came, and they'll remember that meeting. It had been the first meeting in the area, and we held it. From that moment on people ceased to be frightened of saying what they wanted.

Bob the trader

It wasn't my idea to stand for election again. We were
building an organisation. House meetings every night.
Preparing petitions. We were very busy. Bob said Arthur
was quite wrong to call that big public meeting a
shambles: it had been a great success, stirred the area,
brought the people out and now you want to stand for
election. Next month. You might get in. Prove yourself at
public poll. I'll be your agent. Gee them up: they'll be shit
scared. This is the year of decision. You're no pipsqueak
now. He was right. Good old Bob.

I'd known him from the 54-Labour-Party rebel gang
days, in the ghost pub. Bob was a kind of Dutch Uncle to
me, a surrogate brother. He was forever egging me into
stunts, and then letting me down, so I had to do it myself.
I'm not complaining. That's what elder brothers do. I used
to think he had pots and pots of lolly but I don't suppose
he did. He was just a warehouse manager then. I once
had to go to the mill where he worked and he'd a bleeper
on his overalls. Walky talky. The first man I ever saw
with a personalised radio was Bob.

He moved into a magnificent flat in the Park, an ultra-
posh area: private, gated roads and beautiful, curved
gaslamps; a very elegant apartment just beneath the
Castle. I'd call there — forever tapping money, and he'd
rarely lend me any. But he was always buying and selling
things: shirts, curtain fabric. Bob was a trader, though he
was very left wing, his instincts were trading, an eye for
a bargain, nothing for nothing. Arthur pathologically
hated him. Bob was left wing, very, and brazen and
Yorkshire blunt, and he knew everybody in town. He
wore striped shirts, smoked cheroots and drove cars
loudly. In a later generation he might have had a
moustache and jeans — but Bob didn't. He was clean
shaven, often wore a suit and a snappy tie. His own car

was a battered Mini Estate. It was unwashed, strewn with smart and dirty shirts, other people's calling cards, newspapers, periodicals and boxes of this and that and it went bang, bang, up the road. He laughed a great deal — that was why I liked Bob so much — he laughed a great deal whenever anything went wrong. And that's what upset Arthur: he wasn't serious.

Bob also had this knack of being right. He was very bombastic and he could always flatten your beer. You'd hear some good news, and Bob would point out that there was a catch in it, and tell you. There was always a dirty tale behind the scenes that Bob knew: a hidden reason for every good deed. Arthur absolutely hated him. Never let him into his house, and never come up the allotment. They met at meetings, on the street and in campaigns. I had Bob with me as a pal. He called Arthur, Arthur, and would blaspheme in front of officials and people's wives. Not intentionally, but naturally: a smart man with a rough tongue and no apology. Never said sorry. Bob was my friend.

Good old Bob — he eventually ran away with an amazingly beautiful, long-legged girl from the upper echelons of English society. She'd gone revolutionary, and off they went together, fomenting in Latin America in the wake of Che Guevara and that French lefty whose name I forget. They had many escapades and, when they returned to England, they set up a business of world connections, buying and selling school textbooks. It seemed to make money by using a telephone. There was a warehouse in Yorkshire and a grange in Oxfordshire belonging to her family. A proper little squire he became. Good old Bob — you'd phone and a maid would answer, "They're in America." My sour grapes. I seem to have missed that revolution. When half the world were expanding their bodies and minds, blowing their minds out, I was panting up slate strewn streets with a rat in a plastic bag, trying to find some pitiful councillor I could embarass. "We've found this in Dame Agnes Street," you'd say, just as they were going into a civic munch. And Bob led me up to these stunts. He egged me on in the beginning to do things in the slums outrageously, while he was chatting up colonial freedom fighters — liberators. I knew someday somebody would say, come to Cuba, Bob, as surely as I knew some day the Rotary would say to me, be our speaker about housing problems.

Big stir

And so I ran for election again. I knew a lot of people in the district. After two years of shopping, pub crawling and now the big meeting in my belt, I knew a lot of faces, but I didn't know that many people by name, and I panicked — wanting to be popular and egged on by Bob. I went for stunts again, when I could have been serious in a popular cause. It was a terrible mistake.

I was coming up Peas Hill Road, canvassing up this long, narrow, straight street, when I called in the King Edgar for a jar. I introduced myself and a man challenged me: had I been to Enoch Terrace and seen the dumped cars? They had tried the Town Hall, the Labour, the police, the Conservatives, the rat catcher, Uncle Tom Cobbleigh and all. Nobody could shift these dumped cars. Bob said, "Our Ray will. Vote Gosling the tenants' candidate who gets things done." What shall I do, I whispered to Bob. He said "We're trooping everybody out," and out of the pub went everyone, bar the landlord, to Enoch Terrace. There Bob persuaded the strong to push and pull the wrecks on to the main road. "Come on! Heave ho!" Four of us then bundled into a public phone box and I dialled the police. An obstruction on the road. "Who's calling?" and I put the phone down and went — back to the King Edgar. A few minutes later the police called round the houses.

"Does anybody know about these cars on the road, blocking the traffic?'

Nobody blabbed. Nobody told on us. The cars were shifted. I was the toast of the pub. To the terrace a hero, but the terrace wasn't hero in the street. Many tut tutted: disgusting: direct action.

Dorothy heard about it. Now Dorothy didn't drink. She was a woman without a man, with a daughter without a man — and a grandson. She had a house. There were cousins, friends, a sister, enemies, lodgers, a string of allotment gardens in her name and a shed of machettes and a network of burnt out cases to run errands for Dorothy — to hire as favours to fix things for people. You want something? — she was the lady to see. Dorothy was a big lady in an apron. Always something brewing on the stove, forever stewing chicken bones. She was a lady confessor to an empire of backstreet contacts and scandalous information.

Dorothy got us a room for our campaign headquarters on the main drag, in a prime position, in what had been a shop but was now the dusty front room of an unemployed man's lodgings whose wife was well known by the neighbourhood, and by all the passers-by on the bus. She was a very bonny girl with the plumpest pair of bristols ever seen.

We held "surgeries" every night in the shop. Arthur did two nights, six to eight. There was always a queue of people. We plastered the window with news. Whenever we were in the papers we'd Sellotape the cutting. The window was covered in Sellotape. Dorothy wouldn't sit in the shop — but she came down. She'd storm down — often in a temper with an amazing story. "I think you'd better come and have a look at this old lady *now*. She's been hoarding treasure: I've found sackfuls of silver beneath her bed." The end of the back streets were banging all the secrets out. Dorothy was persuading this lady it would be safe to put several thousand pounds of silver coins in a bank.

There was another occasion. Down she came with Mrs Chambers in tow. "You want to improve these houses Gosling — you can't. You're stark, staring mad. I'll show you now." It was the blind end of a terrace. A widow living alone, going out to work and coming home at nights. No running water, but a bucket beside her bed to catch the rain through the hole in the roof. She had to borrow a kettleful from Dorothy's sister, Mrs Chambers's tap, whenever she wanted tea. Other people's drains had seeped up and her garden was a marsh. She'd stepping stones to the front door and no electricity. It had failed and the electric men wouldn't restore it. Unsafe. I was presented to her like I was Aladdin. She looked at me: "Get me out," she said and burst into tears. Dorothy put her arm round her: "There; let's see what he can do." I went to fetch Arthur, there and then, raised him out of his house. "We'll get her out," he said; "I'll write a letter to the councillor tonight." Arthur wouldn't use the telephone. Dorothy said, I will, and Bob turned up. Who said: "We will. We'll do a candlelight procession. I'll phone the papers now. Go and buy yourself some candles, Ray."

The trouble with all these stunts was, again, as we walked the streets with our candles in our hand, big crowds came out to watch us. Some cheered us on but you could hear others mumbling, "That woman — she needs to cry — she poked the hole in the roof herself." And then they'd shout, "You didn't know that. She doesn't deserve rehousing." It was like a Greek chorus screaming at us from the side of the street. "Come and see the hole in my roof, mister. I didn't do mine, I can tell you." We got the woman rehoused, but not until after the election and then it was Arthur's councillor who tricked us and got all the publicity. Bob was away that week. Dorothy was furious.

May Day parade Bob said, "Think of something." Up on the allotments. Arthur said to me, this is all going too far. It's a trap — don't take part. Dorothy said, I'll give them May Day parade. A little kiddy got hurt on Truman Street corner only yesterday. I saw it with my own eyes. All these derelict buildings beginning to fall over. Rubbish on every bit of wasteground. We got no parks where our kiddies can play.

"Get a wheelbarrow, Dorothy," said Bob.

"I've got two on the gardens," said Dorothy. "Our Steph you fetch them down."

And we painted a placard and loaded the barrows with rubble. We painted, "Remove the rubble from St Anns and clean our filthy streets" and when the Labour May

Day procession passed by we tagged along at the end —
Dorothy, Bob, me, a few children and two wheelbarrows.

We got to the Town Hall and had our pictures taken.
Bob wasn't in the picture. He never was a publicity
seeker for himself, but by then he'd had to go somewhere
else. The policeman said, "Now you've had your picture
taken you can take that rubbish back where it came
from." Dorothy said not on your nelly, officer — and there
was a royal row. Dorothy could really raise a ruckus.
She'd been in the Land Army in the war. And in the end
a police inspector phoned the dustbin department who
came and cleared the mess up on condition I accepted a
bill. It's your election, said Dorothy. And we wheeled the
barrows back. It was a rather pathetic ending. I always
seemed to feel a fart at the end of these escapades.

We weren't the only ones doing stunts. There was
Jimmy Green the window cleaner and he was a
councillor, standing for Labour in the markets' end — not
my ward but still the slum district. Harlaxton Street,
phase 10, terrible conditions: a prime example of needing
to be pulled down now. If it really had been worst first,
Harlaxton Street would have been demolished in the
Boer War. Jimmy Green got all the broken down walls
and rubble built into a barricade across the road. The
siege of Harlaxton Street. "We're fed up with the way
they let areas deteriorate," said Jimmy. It blocked the
road. Some of that rubble is privately owned, said the
City Engineer. The police said they'd have to charge
Jimmy with obstruction and he was cautioned. But
nothing happened until after the election. And Jimmy
didn't get back in.

I set the pace in my ward but I didn't get in either. The
sitting Labour (government) candidate was defeated. I
came third. Eleven per cent again. And the Tory was
victor, a new man, by a big margin. I'd had the news,
crowded meetings, great enthusiasm — and no more
votes for my sincerity than I got for my lunacy. I became
the rabble rousers' friend. I was heart-broken. So was the

Labour man. If people who'd voted for me had voted for him, he would have retained his councillor's seat. He wouldn't speak to me for years after that. And a good chapel man. He never got his seat back.

For the act of having been my agent, good old Bob was expelled from the Labour Party for life. His arch enemy, Alderman Roland Green, said, "That's the last nail in his coffin." Bob was absolutely delighted. He'd been pissed off with the Labour Party after two years of Harold Wilson, and now he was going out in style. Bob was bound for anti-apartheid, stop the seventies' South African cricket tour and the world. Before he left he organised a dance. He called it the Sugar Cane Dance and it was one of the rare big dances I've ever been to where grannies like Dorothy and Olive came as well as tarts and intellectuals and big black women like Miss Josie and all the young — black and white, hippie and square and rockers and mods. It was something the English once had when dances were held in country towns. We've lost it completely. Bob organised the dance when everyone was there — except Arthur.

Arthur said, if they'd seen the light and had the sense to throw him out, the Labour Party can't be all bad. Just what does he do for a living? Dorothy was to enjoy the dance and be entwined with Bob in selling this and that for some years — and she turned her spleen on me. I was finished — doing so badly when everything was set up to do well. Of course if she had stood, as she suggested, she would have got in. I said everyone knew we'd lost our credence because of that lady in the shop with the bristols. Everyone knew. I didn't. Arthur said he couldn't divulge how he voted, but the Tories had categorically promised to save his house. And George the Co-op milkman who nominated me said, I didn't vote for you in the end. I decided I couldn't desert the Labour Party as they were bound to lose. But I'm sure we're all glad you stood. The sporting instinct.

Dorothy had been fighting for a school crossing. Bob had brought this lady with a hat — a very posh lady who said she was paid to help us. She talked about children and creche playgroups and mothers' bunny clubs or something, Dorothy said. Anyway she wanted to come to one of our main committee meetings. Arthur said, if she's a friend of Bob's the answer is no. Bob said, she's no friend of mine. I said, I don't want her. I'm fed up. We've got things to talk about among ourselves. And I think I should leave you. Arthur said, standing for election had been most foolhardy. Everyone agreed — except Bob. He said he'd enjoyed it, it had got Ray and our names known, and brought us all together as some kind of a team and the publicity we had was enormous. No matter what they might say both political parties would now be watching us. I said, I want to go: let me out. Arthur said, you're not. We're forming this association properly and you're going to be the chairman. I said no. We compromised; I was co-chairman. George the milkman was my co.

The council wouldn't talk to us, but I'd written a pamphlet and it was published by the Civic Society, full of information we'd picked up — the students' technical details. It was thorough enough for council officials to want to talk to us at the highest level. And then I was sued. Me and Bob had campaigned against a large slum landlord (a public school). We'd handed out leaflets to the children as they were going into school. It was me and a mate called Steve who got done. Bob escaped again. And it was libel — because in fact the school only owned the land, the freehold ground rent and not the houses themselves. I didn't know at the time — but the school were interested in rebuilding houses on their land. It could have been an alternative to the council owning everything. But you live and learn. I had to eat a lot of humble pie. My first apology published in the paper, at my expense, wasn't profuse enough, and I had to bow lower and eat more humble pie and apologise again to that public school.

Dorothy was with these mothers. What had happened was this — children were being taken to school by hand across a nasty road. It was not a busy road, it was nasty because it's on a steep hill and near one of those parks, darkened for generations by rumours of goblins and lurkers. The mothers had written to Honest John — everyone knew Honest John the councillor. They wrote asking for a warden, a lollipop man to see the children safely across the road. See to it, said Honest John. See to it, you did, didn't you John? You instigated an official inquiry — that was the word, "instigated" — men with papers and pads stood around one rainy day taking note of the traffic ebb and flow, and policemen in plain clothes patrolled the lurkers' parks. Officials weighed this evidence and presented their report to the council in confidence, behind closed doors the committee pondered the report, and weighed the costs and pressures and said: no.

Now, Honest John, he told the mothers the news and the mothers said: nesh on you, John, but bless him he tried — and he certainly had tried. Time passed. No child was killed, nearly but not; no child was injured, nearly but not; no child was molested, not even nearly. But the mothers had met with Dorothy present and Bob and this lady with a hat from the Council for Voluntary Service. She was listened to politely and left a lot of pamphlets about doing good to children in poorer areas.

Time passed: until one wet afternoon after the election a prowler nearly snatched a little girl into his car. So it was said. Shame, said the mothers and the school in the next section, they've got five lollipop men. We've counted five and we want one, said the mothers. And the fathers said you'll not get one, now you've had the inquiry. Pipe down. Said the mothers, we'll see. There was much feeling. Emotion and determination ran high. The word spread and Dorothy was recalled. She pulled in her chin and puffed out her chest, put her macintosh over her apron and walked to the school to see all the mothers at coming out time. And she saw they were cross. "Dorothy," they said, "you're on this committee now. Do something."

Well, said Dorothy. And after the children had been put to bed she mentioned these matters to me and to Bob. The following day a gaggle of mothers went into a phone box and rang the newspapers. A child had been molested. Wacko, said the newspaper and they splashed it. The Chief of Police was alerted. The boss of all the schools asked for a comment. The headmistress and the teachers and the council men were running round saying, trust me, trust me, we must have a look again — is the photographer here?

Mm, thought Dorothy. Not enough. A stunt was needed. We'll bring the telly down. We'll start our own warden, she said to the mothers, and Bob brought Dorothy wood and paint. We all held the wood as she painted homemade signs. "Let's paint a zebra on the road," I cried. Hold that sign still, said Dorothy. One she painted **Stop** and the other said **We want a lollipop man**. Bob produced some white gloves and coats, and Annie Din found a peaked cap. They phoned the television and the television came with a mobile van, a cameraman. Action!

Hold it, hold, hold it, said the editor of telly news. Democracy decrees: all sides of the story, both ends of the rope, and he phoned the boss of all the schools — comment, counterpoint the public demands — and the boss of all the schools said: we shall certainly instigate an inquiry, a further inquiry, fully, for these are serious matters — and the head policeman said, aye, aye, and Councillor John said, yes indeed, a very just grievance, and he wore his best shirt, and everyone felt sorry when the news didn't use him.

But on the news in their white coats and peak caps were the mothers, and Dorothy holding their signs and looking unglamorous and speaking in good native tongue. And one of the bosses certainly said: something shall be done. It was a big stir.

But no-one listened, really listened to the mothers as quietly and simply they said they were willing to act as lollipop women themselves, if necessary by rota and private subscription for the present time. They understood the economic climate was hard and public money was short. The mothers were rather pleased with themselves. They'd joined together.

Why is it that the Lord Mayor, aldermen and public servants never listen? Rather than help — they want to do it for you. And these were Tories at a Tory time. They could have said we'll give you coats and you patrol. See how you get on. Have faith. Think not of other things — union agreements, precedents and safety regulations. Bend a little your ear and eye. Take a draught at the fountains of humanity and if you get wet, don't worry, summer will come — whether the council ayes it or no, summer will come.

To another meeting Dorothy brought several ladies in hats and she talked of a mothers' club, a parent-teacher association, playgroup, babysitter service, this crèche — is that right? Dorothy had listened. We found a church hall, the old church hall of the first public meeting, and we hired it and began our first playgroup. Of course the issue of the moment was the lollipop man, and four times daily for two wet weeks the mothers took turns to patrol with their homemade signs. Motorists were amused. The mothers enjoyed themselves. Of course, said Honest John in confidence to all and sundry, this demonstration will prejudice the new inquiries. It is not in your favour to continue it. You have made your point and very well, if I may say so. Don't force the hand which foots the bill. Stop getting wet and looking silly and embarrassing people. And it was wet weather. The fathers were ribbing. Those pictures in the newspapers — you do look bedraggled. And Honest John is a man of wisdom and trust. Who is this Bob?

I saw Honest John in the street. He looked at his diary. "I'm not on that committee... you must understand, it does take time. I suppose it'll have to go before the subcommittee. Am I on that? If..." And he flashed his municipal diary. "So many committees are meeting every day for something..." After the second try, he got us the lollipop man. Honest John got the word **Stop** agreed to be painted on the road beside the school and I found a confectioner in Great Yarmouth to make us 1,000 gobstoppers with the word **Stop** on them like Blackpool rock. The men thought we were bloody bananas. Dorothy had wanted one six foot round treacle **Stop** sign that'd stickyup the cars. The little ones we gave away, and out of that for us, came our first offspring, the first colony of our empire — this flourishing playgroup we ran for many years.

The battles

The Tories won the election, but only the architect changed. Flush with victory they held a meeting, and promised paradise. They took one plank from our platform and named a date — but for total, total destruction: Stan, the most sensible councillor, put forward 1976 for completion. It wasn't popular. People wanted down now, not in nine years' time. We didn't think they could do it by 1976. We were wrong. We also wanted dates for individual terraces. And dates for starting some improvement of the better property. Impossible.

I didn't go to the meeting. Arthur went along. They said, same as the other party, they'd build a new town within the city — and they were cheered. It would be what people wanted and they were cheered. "No budgie boxes in the sky," was their slogan. That was popular. They didn't like architecture. Arthur was disgusted, not that he liked architecture, but "they're Conservatives," he said to me on the allotment. "They promised to save my street, but it's still included in all their maps with the demolition and they won't save anybody else's street." They won't let you down, Arthur, I said, and they didn't.

People had cared for one another in old St Anns but it was breaking. If no-one would go short of a bob or two — there were now exceptions. The cat woman. She wouldn't move into a flat. She stayed in her old house. Her stubbornness was holding up demolition, officials told the neighbours. I said we must help her. Arthur said, it's too extreme and Dorothy for once agreed with Arthur. She'd twenty, maybe thirty cats. She needed a house. She wanted a new one, like everybody else, but she was hounded out of her wits and her cats to death. It was dreadful. She didn't get rehoused. She skulked away and went to live in ruins, coming out on to the street and spitting at people. Five years ago I saw her. She was still

214

alive. An old crow in rags. She recognised me. Her skin was grey but her eyes were bright. "They called me the cat woman," she spat at me; "Your friends, the children, killed my cats."

I'd gone along with the reforming of our organisation after the election, as much to spite those who soothsayed me as a seven day wonder, but it was with some bitterness. I wanted to support Mr Lofthouse. He'd written me, wanting our help to let him stay. He had real sensitivity and his life made sense. Mr Lofthouse lived, simply, alone in National Terrace which was next to St Leger Terrace, racing cul-de-sacs off one of the worst of the worst of the bad back streets. Nobody had a bath in National Terrace, nor an inside lavatory, nor hot running. But Mr Lofthouse kept himself clean at the slipper bath, and a lady did for him at the public washhouse. He was very spruce. The washhouse was much cheaper than the all night commercial laundrettes. You got a good soak, he'd tell me. I tried it. You certainly did. It was an experience in the public baths. A deeper way of washing.

Mr Lofthouse's house was very small. You had to bend your head a lot. It was spartan, but clean and rat free. He did for himself when he came home from work. He didn't drink. He read a lot and watched TV. He wanted his house, which he rented at 7/6d a week, to stay up. He didn't want to shift. He liked being close to the slipper bath. He didn't want *any* improvements, except a better streetlight on the corner.

Would he organise a petition, I asked, to see how many others on the terrace were like him and wanted to stay? "Oh," he said, "what would a petition involve?" I explained. "Oh," he said, "would his landlord or the foreman at work find out about it?" Did that matter said I. "Oh," he said, looking at me sheepishly. There was a long pause. "I suppose not," he said in a whisper. He promised to try. He said there was a Pole across the way who might sign. He couldn't vouch for the others.

215

To his credit, he mustered the courage and called on his neighbours with the petition. I'd typed the heading — and he did call on all his neighbours. There were three signatures wanting to stay up out of twenty houses on the terrace.

"I had rude replies," he said, "from some of the women in the houses who wouldn't sign. They were very rude. I appreciate why they refused, but why did they abuse me? Will they tell my foreman? You see for me, National Terrace suits me: where will I get another home — it's a shelter — and where will I get another at 7/6d a week so close to a slipper bath?" He looked at me sheepishly. "In the end it will come down won't it?'

I said, I'll fight — we'll fight, Mr Lofthouse. But I didn't. Not well enough did I champion Mr Lofthouse's cause. I let him down. He was my first compromise. Arthur wouldn't let me support him. His terrace wasn't worth saving. We'd be a laughing stock. We must be sensible.

At the first public inquiry I did my first dirty trick. The landlord of Mr Lofthouse's house at National Terrace had no objection to being compulsorily purchased and the house demolished. I should have spoken for the tenant, for Mr Lofthouse. In those days tenants couldn't speak only owners. Public inquiries were property inquiries. But I had won the right of representation: I could have spoken. The inquiry was packed with people we'd encouraged to come, but they all wanted, every Jack and Jill of them to be out now, down quick. To have spoken for Mr Lofthouse, for cheap living, I think I'd have been lynched.

My committee thought so and I was instructed to restrain my silly side. Our organisation had to be taken seriously. Public officials up-town were talking to us. We were being taken seriously because of the detail in the students' plans. Because I'd produced this pamphlet. Because we were still getting fed information by middle-grade officials. Because the inspectors who control public inquiries are from central government, federal men. We were given respect.

My committee were flattered at the flannel. The door may not have opened more than ajar but we were whispering through a lot of keyholes. Councillors wouldn't speak to us, not officially. Because of me standing at an election. We arranged a meeting with them for a Sunday but only one turned up — a lovely Conservative lady who wore big hats and had a rich plummy voice and was the one to go to nick later for fiddling dead men's votes. The rest wouldn't turn up — "Not on a Sunday," said the press. "Not with him," they said on the radio — not with me. I spoke to the lady about Mr Lofthouse privately. She was sympathetic but there was nothing she could do — and cheap living was swept away in the rush of redevelopment. The right of man to live cheap on his own account, from his own resource, without a subsidy — that was the first chopping of the wood to make the gallows that were to hang working class culture as the back streets knew it.

Today in my district the only way a working man can live cheap is by ceasing to work and claiming social security. A distinctive way of life is extinguished. Poor but honest. Small but proud. Cheap — no more. I should have stuck by Mr Lofthouse — but no-one supported me. We were testing a students' thesis, we were building an organisation, we were letting the masses speak — we were not collecting freaks. We were to ride the tide not row against it.

Absolute hullabaloo

The council opened an official advice bureau in an old shop. They had queues in the street but ours got busier, correcting and presenting arguments to what the council men said. We sold our pamphlet. It wasn't very popular among the people. The council produced a pamphlet. It had a glossy picture on the front, a really romantic photograph of steam coming out of a manhole cover on the curve of an old cobbled street. Real romance of the slums — but the title of their pamphlet was *Towards Renewal*. And inside it was all New Jerusalem. Where have all the cobbles gone, and the iron gaslamps, and all the old street plaques? — to the suburbs every one. The romance of the slums. I haven't kept any. Not even from where my granny came from. I suppose I should have done. I had plenty of chances and they'd be worth something today. They had a craftsmanship in them. In a cobble — yes.

Arthur said, why is it these new electric lamps are left on all night and often all day? There used to be a little gasman who'd walk the old streets with a key on a pole and turn a tap, so everything went off at dawn.

And just then what proved to be the big boulder of publicity dropped into the pond. My old pals from the ghost pub, Ken and Billy, the sociologists, produced their pamphlet — with stark and stunning photographs they declared our area poverty struck. It made the biggest splash. By saying very simply, like the boy in the Hans Christian Andersen fairy tale: look everybody, this district is dreadful — an appalling, festering slum. Poor people are living in filth and squalor and poverty — families are, the children are — and with statistics they proved it. They also wrote with some style: "Perhaps the trips to the outside lavatories encourage community contact."

That, like the discovery of life on an uninhabited planet, let loose all hell and the ballyhoo of public opinion. Like a goldrush, national experts rushed to the district. The measuring men, the newshounds, the government promised to support. Politicians and pundits toured the area in charabancs, the equivalent of senators on fact finding tours. It was as if an earthquake had hit. The area's moment had come. School-children in the posh suburbs collected food parcels. One school sent us £250. Jean Malone came rushing down to the shop. "There's a man," she said, "promising free ice-cream to all the children if they go to the Forest next week and clear the streets. It's the Army. They're going to use our derries, our old back streets, as a training ground for Northern Ireland." We'll stop them. We did.

Architects worked through the night to design only the quickest for our poor people's future. Big builders formed consortia to offer packages of the swiftest in housing. Planners' heads were trimmed. Politicians' promises glowed, in the twilight like a morning star. There was an old Co-op leader with a gammy leg who wisely said at the time: "Beware promising people Father Christmas." But Father Christmas was what they got. And hadn't they waited long enough? They were deserving poor with the chance of a lifetime. People now scrambled over one another to prove their house was worse than the house next door. People lit fires in their homes, and some were lucky: they burnt to the ground and were the quicker rehoused. The moment was theirs. The world that mattered was listening.

The sociologists — "poverty mongers" — first produced their pamphlet, then a booklet, then a best selling Penguin paperback. Then there was a television film. We felt increasingly impotent, and jealous at being picked on for our poverty. I challenged Ken and Bill to come and talk to us. They wouldn't. Why should they? — they were talking to the world. We tried to get some counter publicity for our attempts to raise ourselves up, to show we weren't a passive poor but had some fight in us. It was useless. The bad news of the poverty was so riveting — but it hurt us. We were the rivets.

Mick on the committee went to work the morning after the first showing of the poverty film on television and there was a piece of string on his lathe. "What's this?" "For you, you poor bogger, you live down there where the kids all tie their shoes with string."

I was doing a weekly television show, of a different kind, by then. I went to talk to the local Rotary. I said, what shall we talk about? — my telly or this district I'm involved with? The district, the slum, oh yes please, said the Rotary and they all leant forward. That was the matter of the moment. Poverty was what they wanted to hear.

People were moving in, from miles around, into our district, to rent crabby rooms in charred terraces knowing once there, their plight would be attended to. If you were poor and could you made for our district. It's famous for it. The council men in charge of property were wising up too late. As soon as one family was rehoused, another moved in. Fill 'em up, we cried.

The future was coming. The odd thing was, we were waiting for them to provide, at a time of increasing affluence and increasing freedom. Isn't that odd? Couldn't we clear the bad parts of the slum without the council? Couldn't we improve anything? Over the hill, around my rotting villas, people were borrowing money easily all over the shop to improve their own homes. I feared the future. Rarely have we taken a poor district that was, with all its faults, human and happy and in making its housing clean and decent not made as a by-product so many lonely people, unhappiness in tidy homes, created delinquency in the young and depression in the old. Those with initiative got the hell out.

For a long time, it was as if people and council combined in an unspoken alliance to vandalise and make matters worse. Landlords as a class were killed off. They got scant compensation. The council was buying the area in the fastest, cheapest compulsory purchase they could, and this was a Conservative council. It was priority number one. There was now a timetable of action. The Jeremiahs, including me, said it couldn't be done. But it was, and within the time. People rehoused: an area of 30,000 people utterly changed, according to schedule.

Having an affection for the rum life of seething backstreets, and fearing the uniformity that would take their place, I thought that a few of the better old houses should be kept and retained. They were, kept, improved and changed from private to council ownership, and made as modern and spick and span as the new. Everyone wanted the new. Plastic furniture that children's heads wouldn't bang on. Change came like a torrent sweeping all before it: houses, streets, chapels, shops, pubs, the whole old life. Not only the face of the neighbourhood changed but the body and spirit of the people: the constitution, grit and social composition. A history was wiped away.

Building an army

We still held the holy book of the students' plans. They finished their thesis, passed their exams and we put an exhibition of their ideas in our shop window. They seemed a little academic now: the case for selective renewal and improvement of an area that was beyond hope. That's progress. Selective renewal. It has succeeded in smaller schemes. Public officials on the spot and local builders giving encouragement to people to help themselves. Having a municipal direct works department, there with spare parts, like a do-it-yourself shop. Make and mend. The council giving technical advice. Encouraging self respect. Building up home enterprises. But it was too late for us. Our slum was too big. It had been declining a long time. The students were hard-headed and without my sentiments. They believed it could be done — even in St Anns — but the will had gone.

Dorothy, ever inventive, found me a house and I moved in — 5 Brighton Street — to have a last ditch effort at improving an old place myself. You couldn't get an improvement grant. I got no support and failed miserably. The only small builder who would help gave a plastic bath: all the others would only sell. I couldn't plumb it up without paying. The hardware shops were all selling up, complaining only to up their compensation. I felt the chance slipping through my hands like sand. When the books are written they'll clearly show how capitalism deserted the Conservative working class — it abandoned backstreet people to a Wimpey-built, council house estate: that people be consumers, for mass production, for a conglomerate institution's profit.

In many towns when an old slum has to be demolished, the community is broken up, scattered and the land cleared. What was a living neighbourhood becomes a sad and derelict site for years until a new development rises and a new community is settled on the fallow land. In the 1950s and 1960s swathes of our cities from Glasgow to Portsmouth lay fallow. We were one of the last slums to be dealt with, and we didn't want that to happen to our district. We wanted to keep our community as far as we could. We wanted the new housing to be built as soon as the site was cleared, because a lot of our people — not all, but a lot — wanted to stay in the district, close to town where they'd friends.

I also wanted us to choose our new world. That it wouldn't be something foisted on us. That the people would be clients and directly have a say in the design of the new. The Tories in power kept telling us to look at Wimpey houses. It soon became obvious why. In the general euphoria to speed the scheme for our district, council politicians were going to give the first rebuilding contract to Wimpey.

I always passed by the china stall kept by Ron, the Tory councillor, even when he wasn't speaking to me. I think we were quite fond of each other, or maybe I'm just romantic. Anyway, he spoke to me one week after the pound had been devalued.

"Hello, Ray, I'm not speaking to you... you're political. How are things?... Shouldn't have stood you know. I know who your friends are. You can't fool me. We won't speak to you till you stop being political." Pause. "Wicked Labour government, isn't it now — how can you be a socialist after Wilson's devalued the pound?"

He then said, the leader of the council wants to see me. Make up a small deputation and come to his room in Town Hall on Saturday at noon. And we did. The leader said, how evil the socialists were we couldn't conceive. There wouldn't be any development if it wasn't for the Conservatives and the socialists tried to sabotage every scheme to bring progress to the people. Would you care for a drink? I said no, sanctimonious prig I was then. All the rest said yes.

Now, have you seen any Wimpey houses? We said we had: we'd been organising bus trips all over, to every kind of new development around, and even up to Rochdale, because we wanted house like houses. He gathered himself together. I could see he was intrigued. Trips — tenants taking trips to see new house designs. He carried forward. Exactly, and the leader slapped his thigh. You'll have seen, so you'll know Wimpey houses are not budgie boxes in the sky, now are they? Admit it? We were silent. The leader was a rough, stocky avuncular man, with a thick handlebar moustache that curled, and black hair set in waves around his big ruddy face, wreathed in smiles. He repeated his literary phrase. No, we shan't have budgie boxes in the sky that I can promise you. He knew where he was going.

Why, we squeaked up, can't we have contracts given to small local builders? He leant forward and looked at us intently. I wish they could, he said, from the bottom of my heart. But they can't do the job you see — it's too big for the little men.

We said, we like brick tradition, and Wimpey's houses are concrete. He looked at us: "Can't get bricklayers for love nor money, the more's the pity." Then turning to one of his aides he said, "I suppose they could have brick hangings: tiles that look like bricks stuck on the concrete." Oh, and we all beamed. It was the inspiration of the moment. "Wouldn't that be nice," I think I said, "tiles that look like bricks — in different colours?" "Yes," he said, "I suppose so. I don't see why not in different colours."

Why can't the council demolish really bad houses now, we said. "I know," and he told us a childhood story of his own hard times, and of the storm that ended in a rainbow.

"You see, it has to be phase by phase, done by numbers because big contractors need large cleared sites before they can start. There can be no bitting and bobbing about. People must patiently wait their turn. It is inevitable, there will be suffering which is why we are pressing on with the scheme in such haste, and the wicked socialists are hampering our every effort."

It was a superb performance. We were sunk into heavy leather chairs, he behind a desk; us with drinks, he without; his aides at his elbow.

What about good houses on the edge of the area, and factories and workshops, I said, can't they be saved? Do they have to be all knocked down?

He looked at his aide: "Are there many on the edge? Because if there are we might be able to do something if they're on the edge. It might save us some money."

I opened a map, and spread it across his desk. "A map!" he stood up. "Yes, let me see." I'd coloured our map just like the planners do, only with colours for the things we wanted done.

"You lend us your map, my boy, and I promise on Monday morning, first thing, I shall ask my officers to look into this because this could save ratepayers' money and in these days of devaluation, when loans are in jeopardy, due to the mess the evil socialists have got this country into..."

We came out of that meeting so elated. I think we nearly hugged one another. Arthur thought his street was really saved, and it was a breakthrough, for from that moment on civil servants and councillors all chatted us up. We'd got the leader's ear. There was a bright architect in the City Architect's office who came to see us. The redevelopment couldn't just be given to Wimpey, it had to go out to tender, so there was a chance it could be better, or other than Wimpey. Would we look at his scheme? We were flattered and excited. It was better than Wimpey, in brick, it could be built by local builders. But it would have taken longer, and time had been lost. Speed was the word. Wimpey won the contract, and to be fair they acted on lots of our suggestions. They gave us some more kit for our tenants' advice shop. But having got the first contract, and their building machines installed, they easily won every other contract, every phase until the last.

By the time of the last phase, the Labour Party were back in power. They had a new architect commissioned to design something different — with courtyards, and to be built of black brick — low rise but with imagination. There's a set of flats they call the ski slope because they have a roof that slopes straight from floor three to about six foot from the ground. The trouble was, being in the last phase, there were none of our people left. They were all incomers. And the last phase was on the edge of the area. The Labour Party had it well-designed and half built when the Conservatives came back and in cutting the rates they didn't finish it off: at least not with the detail it needed. Dearie, dearie. It isn't simple, is it?

When I reflect, now looking back, we were wrong to give in to popular panic and let speed override but we had to. Quantity before quality. There was no practical way, in the society we lived in, to stop the tide of speed. Out now, the people cried.

We'd had meetings with Wimpey and the planners. We were against the motorways. We held a public meeting, I remember. It was well and properly advertised, a leaflet in everyone's door, posters in the shops. We wanted to give people the chance to query the design of the new homes, and see the plans so far: to make sure what was built was what they wanted. To our embarrassment more council officials turned up than people. People couldn't care less now about choice.

In the parts we were persuading the authorities to improve there were mutterings against us. They'd have been better off coming down. Improvement took so long. Landlords were so reluctant. There was one sector where the church owned the land — the Church of England. And they could not agree with the council. They wouldn't improve the houses they owned themselves unless A, B, C, D *et cetera* were done. And they wouldn't sell to the council, for the council to improve unless X, Y, Z *et cetera*

226

were done and the twain never met. We lobbied the churches: did we interrupt their services? It was embarrassing. When we did a district meeting, it was fifty-fifty wanting to stay up/come down and we swung it to stay up and be improved with our pressure on the council of the time — and then nothing happened. With improvement there could be no compulsion. There was no Wimpey-like big contractor, or direct works department geared up to do improvement with speed. The council were buying older houses to put problem families in. They were practising participation exercises in improvement areas to the point of procrastination. I remember a widow came to see me with the latest council improvement brochure in her hand: "I wanted to be improved," she said, "but on these plans they've put a tree where my front parlour is. I know we need trees, but now we've won improvement has my house got to come down for a tree?"

There was no incentive to stay. Wimpey were so quick to put in the first footings and the place became a battleground: it looked it, physically.

We were doing good works. The students left but I stayed, and out of our energy, or to be more correct, out of our ability to excite other people to energy, grew an empire in our name. We created a real people's organisation — a society that cared from cradle to grave. There were two children's playgroups we were running for the under fives, an adventure playground we were designing, a home in the country, a tote that raised money, care groups for the sick and street stewards for every street. For the elderly there were sixty-plus clubs and lots of outings. And to help us be forever tickling authority we engaged our own full-time worker. The United Nations had found us a young English girl from college to be our first civil servant — to work for us, paid by us from money we raised ourselves. Nothing to do with the authorities. And she invited into our last years as a slum, a whole hippy commune who created a craft centre and workshops, a free food co-operative, an urban farm and a community newspaper and all enterprises blossomed like a tree, and some are still bearing fruit. Some ripened just right. Some fell to the ground in storms before they could be picked — but we built a world, a little soviet ourselves.

We had storms, of course; we were in the business of battle. We fought against everybody, one time or another, and although we fought among ourselves, we took on the world. We fought against the urban motorway and we won. Every day for thirty days and nights I was at that wretched public inquiry — but the road wasn't built. Houses are built and our own boozing club stands on the land that should have been the motorway.

Dorothy got involved with a youth club — she did have this nose, as close to the ground as a mole, and she was born in the district. She'd heard about an old church building that hadn't been used since the 1930s. It had been a working men's tea/cocoa rooms and was closed by the police because they found the old men gambling. Days before casinos were licensed! Dorothy wanted it reopened for youth. The vicar was quite keen, but preferred to stay in the background. There was a Methodist minister who was very keen, a real goer for youth: with most modern ideas. A meeting was called. Probation were there. Child care. Churches. A boxing club. And the Tenants' Association — me, Dorothy and Arthur. Dorothy said we could have table tennis and a tea urn and she knew a man who could organise a football team. Arthur said young people needed discipline. Probation coughed. The minister said, 'oh no, the modern thing was a coffee bar and popular music' — a self-programming youth club they're called and have been tried in Sheffield and in Leicester too. I kept my head down. You've got to attract the kids, and then give them ten minutes of prayer like a commercial break in the middle of the evening. Dorothy wasn't keen on the prayer. She was even less keen on the coffee bar music — and when dim lights were mentioned... Arthur said to me later, on the allotment, and that's Christianity.

I took a back seat in all this. I thought I'd seen this Catherine wheel turn before. The place opened. They engaged a youth leader just as wild as I had been. It was like a re-run. The place ran out of money, and for a rescue operation the British Council of Churches were called. They said they could bail us out, and grant cash. It was a multiracial project: it was, wasn't it? We were the St Anns: with a lot of black people as well as the poverty. Oh yes, we said. They said they'd come up, to see us in person. Oh Crikey.

They came on an announced day, thank God — because at that time, as it so happened the current clientele were what could only be described as Paki-bashers: 100 per cent thick whites. *Ark Boot Boys Rule* they scrawled all over the walls by away football grounds. We hate niggers, I heard them chanting once — in the street outside the Mecca. When the delegation came up, we were very careful what to show them: plenty of black homes and not so long in the club. We got the money. I'd taken the leading role in this public relations exercise. I felt awful. And then for no reason, but it must have been an act of God, before we actually paid the cheque in, the clientele changed overnight to a 100 per cent black reggae youth — just like that. The neighbours didn't like it either way. And one bonfire night the Ark burnt to the ground. There was a new vicar, who had the ruins razed and sown with grass so quick — but you can still see scrawled on the walls opposite *Ark Boot Boys Rule.*

The troops

People wanted to get out, and there seemed only one way now, one power, one almighty provider — the council. I went to see a lady who was an office cleaner in a council department. She was in a late phase, but how could she get out quick? She was desperate. I explained, if she accepted a highrise flat or one on an unpopular overspill estate she would be moved quicker than if she waited for Wimpey to finish their popular homes nearby. But like so many she wanted a house for a house. She was a single woman. Her house wasn't too bad. I was tired and I let slip a thought from the back of my own self-sufficient childhood. I have these thoughts even though I don't/I didn't practise them. I said "If you'd saved the money of course you could *buy* a house."

She looked at me. "I've only got a few thousand saved, but there must be more with my brother who lives with me. He saves. Neither of us drink."

What am I talking to you about council houses for? They had £7,000 between them. There were estate agents who sell houses like ironmongers sell garden forks. But people had forgotten.

Maclean was a black man: an elephant of a black man. He kept his family together in a rotting terrace until his house was the only one standing. To get in and out the family had to climb over the rubble. The council offered them council house after house. The bulldozer came closer and closer. Maclean refused all offers, insisting the council fix him a mortgage loan to buy a new place of his own. And they did, eventually, but what privations that family suffered to get what they wanted. They knew their rights and we supported him. An elephant of courage.

George, the Co-op milkman, who was my co-chairman, took time off and came on all our deputations up-town. He owned his house, a little house, and he fought and we fought with him to keep it up. But it was in an island of reasonable property totally surrounded by bad. It would have made the contractors' life difficult. Earth scrapers wouldn't have got a clear run. But we were winning the argument, when George suddenly announced to the committee one Sunday morning, he was resigning. He'd sold his house out to the council. Made a good price too: the first to fight, the first to give in. With his compensation he found himself a little pub in the country. He did do well. And so did the corporation, for with George gone, the movement to keep that street up collapsed.

There were stupid, sad cases who took the first offer the corporation made. An eighty-year-old lady found herself on the tenth floor of a horrid highrise, because her offer for rehousing came through the post on a day when her only visitor was a timid cousin. It was her first offer but he'd said: "If you refuse, they'll put you out on the streets. Auntie," and she stupidly believed him. She knew about us, but we weren't there on the day. The cousin was. She was frightened, in a panic. No-one was put on the streets, but some officials did say enough to make it a heavy rumour. To give people the strength to stand up for their rights was like forcing castor oil down children, and it had to be done with such regularity.

Elsie was an exception. If Maclean was an elephant of a man, she was an elephant of a woman — but aren't women different kinds of creatures! Elsie lived in an absolute hovel. She picked at the walls to make matters worse. She lived with a mynah bird and many urchin grandchildren. Her face was weatherbeaten and wrinkled. She'd white hair and a stick. She moved slowly in long, dark, voluminous skirts. She looked like a photograph of a very old Victorian woman. She'd either grin or grimace. Elsie wrote to me — childlike-writing and I called. She showed me all over the house. I said it was shocking, and it was. What could I do, precious little maybe but what had she done? Ah, ah! She produced a bundle of letters from Ladies-in-waiting. She'd written to every member of the royal family, more than once: I think all she needed was the Duke of Gloucester for a royal flush. She'd replies from private secretaries to Bishops, from Marcia Williams, and the national leaders of political parties for over a decade. The Queen, if she had visited, could possibly have persuaded Elsie to move. If the Queen had offered her a new house, she might have accepted. But for the rest of us it was more difficult. Whenever she got an offer she turned it down. She'd grin and click her teeth like a naughty princess who'd turned down yet another suitor.

"I'm waiting for the right one. It is shocking where I'm in, in't it? You'll not see as bad as mine. Worst in the street. Worst for miles around. Had a sociologist from university said it was. I'm waiting for the President of the Students' Union. Says he'll call. Written to say he will, he has. I'll show him. I'll show you the letter — see what he can do."

When she did go, Elsie moved just a few streets away, to another old house, on the opposite side of the valley. From its back door, she could take a last, long lingering look at the demolition of what had been her finest hour. Decade. She knew it — and played it like a dying opera queen!

With all the rehousing we lost a lot of good people, and committee people but Dorothy stayed, the big lady, trouble-shooting. She moved like Elsie within the area, from phase to phase, two jumps ahead of the bulldozer, taking part in every battle with relish. She chucked me out of the house I wanted to improve when it was clear I was taking a hiding for nothing — and filling the place with unsavoury lodgers. She was good at that. Moving in and sorting you out whether you wanted it or not. Her and her hangers-on. As once the agents of landlords called on Dorothy to advise them on their little difficulties, so the council now called on Dorothy to help them out with cases that had stretched their patience.

There was Miriam from Festus Street, happy as a sandboy was Miriam, collecting old furniture out of derelict houses and carrying it on her head, African-style, to fill her house and her yard and eventually her whole derelict terrace with tables and chairs, she laid out, as if she were expecting a party of guests, like Tenessee Williams's gentlemen callers. She wouldn't be parted from her possessions and the more demolition, the more possessions, the more she wouldn't be parted.

Dorothy sorted her out. Dorothy now had a friend, Joanne, who was very attentive and bright, and who quickly rose on various committees. She took our minutes very well. Then she had a tiff with Dorothy, or more likely Dorothy had one with her. I didn't pay any attention. One Sunday meeting, there we are in the shop, and Dorothy isn't there. It comes to any other business and Joanne says she must make a personal statement: she felt she'd have to tell the committee, she couldn't go on living a lie. I knew what was coming. I bowed my head and covered it with my hands and out it came — Joanne was a sex change. The tale went on for it seemed an eternity and you could hear a pin drop. Eventually it stopped when Joanne threw herself upon the committee's mercy. I looked up and said well what do we do, and I looked round the room. That's the trick. I'll go round the room. Cast the first stone. Some people hated it, but everyone said what difference does it make? She... er, Joanne takes the minutes very well. But there wasn't one dirty word or smirk and she stayed.

A week or so later the vicar called. Not the nice vicar but the one with the alsatian dog. He called on me at home. He cleared his throat, at the front door. This was confidential business, could we talk in private? I took him upstairs to my workroom. I didn't say anything, and it took him an hour before he reached the point. He took a deep breath in and I knew what was coming. Did you know — this may come as a great shock to you — but I have reason to believe the treasurer of your playgroups using my church hall is not a proper woman. Oh, ah, I said. Really? I said, yes, I knew. What a disgrace, said the vicar. What will the parish council say if this leaks out — and God forbid if the mothers find out. I said most mothers know. And she handles the money not the children, but even if she did she's got children of her own. The vicar put his face in his hands. Good grief — he looked up to me, it must be removed. Not by me, we're happy with Joanne. Said the vicar, I'll write to the Bishop at once, at once, and he pulled at his dog and went away in a hurry, shocked to the marrow because I wouldn't do anything.

I told Joanne what happened. She was furious — a vicar — if that's Christian charity when she was working for playgroups for nothing, she'd jolly well expose the truth about herself in the *News of the World*. What an odd reaction I thought, but our world was full of odd reactions.

Anyway a couple of Sundays later there it is — in the news on the right hand of the front page — "The truth I dare not reveal to my son: I am not his mother but his father" — and one of those rear view pictures of our treasurer in a leather skirt. I looked on the other side of the front page of the *News of the World* and, lo and hobgoblin, it was reported that our Bishop had run off with a showgirl from the Eve club in Soho called Amanda Lovejoy. Talk about truth being stranger than fiction, and there was a quote from the poor Bishop's wife — "I always thought," she said, "he was going to London on Convocation business" — and a quote from the Archdeacon saying this had all come as a shock and the Bishop was a fine man known for his work among young people. He never came back. Church found him some post as chaplain in the Canary Islands and the *News of the World* later had a telephoto picture of him sunbathing on the beach with the admittedly luscious Amanda Lovejoy.

P.S. Our Joanne is still around.

Jesus on a bicycle

There was a lot of empty property towards the end. But we never got squatters. Tramps, dossers, odd people squatting out but never a squatters' movement. Our houses were too poor, too tiny, all too rough. What we did get was some rather special super hippies and I encouraged them.

The girl was Jill, from the *Peace News* tradition. Her boyfriend of the time was nicknamed Jesus, because he had a beard. They walked barefoot in jeans. They didn't believe in money. They gave — kindness and skill and trusted people to provide their food and shelter. The boyfriend was strong. Jill was beautiful. He moved people. She taught reading and writing, sewing and knitting. They refused social security and would never accept money from anyone. They lived on what they received in kind. And they returned in kind. A butcher gave them meat, he was so fond of them — so much meat they had to set up a lunch club to use the excess and provide free meals to old folk. The council gave them an empty corner shop on Bluebell Hill. They charged a peppercorn rent of £1 a week but someone always paid that. There they lived, and set up their commune. They were beautiful. They were real pioneers of a genuine alternative society based on love and self-help rather than profit but, unlike the Women's Institute, their home craft was communal, non-competitive, free and fulltime. Secular friars and sexual nuns. I thought, and I still do, that these hippies were the most, had the most beautiful idea that flowered in the dying days of the slum. They came to what was a prison and made it a playground for their ideas and enthusiasm. They were very attractive people.

Dorothy, one of the old school, was put out. She cared for people, but her network was never attractive. Her lodgers were not beauties and always in trouble. Dorothy had no generous benefactor to pay her rent. No middle class happy home had she left behind. Dorothy's folk had been battered and insecure since childhood. They had to bustle and go through the hassles of social security. The hippies quickly collected, in their commune shop, the biggest permanent jumble sale collection in the district, so Dorothy had to do business with them. A film company made a film of their ideals and enthusiasm and goodness, and it glowed on television screens at Christmas time. A manufacturer gave tons of ice-cream once for the hippies to give to children, while poor Dorothy was stewing apples from her allotment gardens into toffee apples and was threatened with prosecution by public health. The district was becoming an estate, laws were changing and standards rising. Dorothy's network diminished.

Dorothy was always in trouble, her manner bossy. She wouldn't deign to attend ordinary meetings and could never muster that little bit more than a clique you need to vote for you at AGMs, and Dorothy's clique were not the 'point of order Mr Chairman' kind. As our respectability as an organisation increased, and membership grew into card-holding members, more card-holders wanted Dorothy out and off. They rubbed their hands with joy in the street when Dorothy was charged by the police with stealing a plastic sheet from Wimpey. She refused to resign but the committee stood her down. In court she was convicted. On appeal she was acquitted. The committee wouldn't have her back. She left for an overspill estate.

Times were changing fast. The craft centre hippies had held a street eat party with old tables and chairs, Miriam style, and marvellous free eats. It was a wake for a terrace about to be demolished. It was absolutely marvellous, everyone enjoyed it, it went on the front page of the *Guardian* and people talked of a festival, a free festival next year.

Next year the street party was to be held for the first time in one of the new council house squares. There was uproar. The noise had been too loud. There was litter everywhere. People didn't mind the litter in the old terrace but people were paying high rents now, for these new houses, and why were the hippies getting their commune at only £1 a week? Scot-free for some. There was a tremendous fuss. I defended the craft centre and the attack was beaten back. But the hippies' confidence was bruised. Some of them felt unwelcome. They argued among themselves, in the commune and some split to the country, others went to other slums. The battle for our slum was over. The new houses were turning people houseproud. The new rents were making people very jealous. We'd lost the cameraderie of the old cobbled backstreet days. We were losing the mucking-in we had to do when we were fighting for the basic rights of shelter.

We'd lost in seven years 500 small shops and fifty public houses, with their little rooms to hire above the vaults. We'd lost 12,000 open grates and were all centrally heated now, and all the homes owned by the council. There is still poverty, and plenty of grievance. Our committee, the membership, the work continues. But we're on our own — that is the tragedy. All the attention we had as a slum. Now we are a council house estate: our benefactor or enemy, the council. It is a different world.

I wouldn't put the clock back. I was a party to what was done, and it had to be done. But I wish change would come gradually, as it does in middle class districts, in the suburbs, and in normal villages. We had to be razed to the ground because we'd been forgotten by all the multitude of landlords for decades. Now we're in our new world, our council house estate under one almighty authority, we are in danger of being forgotten again.

Death at Christmas

I could go on about the nitty gritty of housing and backstreet/council house life. Maybe I should. But that makes another book — maybe that is the book, but it's not how this book began and there were other things in my life. In 1972 I was making films about places for television. In December I was preparing my commentary for a film about Rochdale — running into the very last days of editing, trying to wheedle into the script everything I wanted to say.

Rochdale is an interesting town: begetter of the Co-op, drab and wet and its people over-friendly but ever so interesting to me because in the cotton mills — they still have them — there are thousands of immigrants working. Ukranians, Filipino girls on contract labour and the Pakistanis — all Muslims. Now I always thought when I was young the immigrants would make an *England Half English* — which is the title of a collection of essays by my mentor, Colin MacInnes. I thought the immigrants would bring calypso bands and colour and freedom and life to our drab industrial towns. It hasn't happened like that in Rochdale. As the native English Nonconformist has faded away, these new arrivals have come along and, particularly the Muslim immigrants, have brought it all back. The spirit of my father. The spirit of hard work, abstemiousness and self-sufficiency. Don't drink. Don't smoke. Don't kiss in the street. Don't marry unless your father approves.

You'd think the children of immigrant parents, Muslim boys and girls born in Rochdale, might rebel like I did — or be corrupted by our now permissive English ways but I found they were not. I met Pakistani schoolgirls spoken for. Ukranian teenagers believing in a strict and moral life. I do envy the immigrants their industriousness. I'm glad I wasn't a child of theirs and I fear for our permissive society.

I'm writing this at home, trying to wangle it into the script in as few words as the pictures will let me. It's not the way to make films. It's not the way I'd like it. I go up to the studios on the train and try to lengthen the picture, then come back home and play with the words. Put away the script for a long weekend of neighbourhood politics, seeing people, of sitting in our community shop taking up the complaints. I did the Saturday morning session. There was a meeting on Sunday. I should have gone there on Monday to talk to Arthur, now secretary, about future moves. I didn't. And on Tuesday morning I learnt on the telephone that Arthur had collapsed, after doing a session at the shop. The Catholic priest had picked him up off the street and he was taken to hospital. I phoned the newspapers. It made the front page. I phoned the Town Clerk to forward all business to me, and then I phoned the hospital. It was clearly serious. They said visitors apart from kin were not allowed. I worked on the Rochdale script, and an article I was preparing on dog racing. But every time I left my desk to make a cup of tea, I swelled up inside, all my senses tense, and yet I slept okay that night.

Wednesday, 20 December, the phone rang at seven a.m. I was half awake when Trevor his son-in-law said he had died. So many to tell, said Trevor, so much to do. He was such a wonderful man, wonderful man — never be another — could I meet the family in the afternoon to talk about the arrangements? I re-dialled, passing the message on to Margaret our community girl that Arthur was dead. She burst into an uncontrollable sob. I just put the phone down. Got dressed. Made a cup of coffee. Worked on the Rochdale script.

When a friend is ill, like yesterday, I wanted to tell the world and get everyone to pray, that was the implication. But now Arthur's dead I want to tell no-one. I want to pretend it hasn't happened. It helps, having to con-centrate on other things, being much too busy with work.

At nine o'clock the phone went again. There was big trouble. Every year we gave free Christmas parcels to our old folk. This year some had got two and some had got none. The old folks were scrapping, and how's Arthur? He's dead, in the night. Oh God! Now about these Christmas parcels... You can't believe it, at ten o'clock there's more phone calls coming in. There's going to be such a fuss at the passing of Arthur. Almost a competition for the best displays of grief and, in the midst of our grief, Sid is calling for an emergency meeting. What an insult to Arthur who built us up, that we're not strong enough to calmly continue. Still we're a family business, but I wish we'd mourned first before plotting who is to fill Arthur's shoes. I've just had a terrible thought — what if the hippies had pushed Arthur down, or the blacks? Folk are only a degree from wanting to avenge this death. None of us expected it, and now I've heard there's to be a post-mortem. Apparently it's normal when a man dies suddenly to have a post-mortem. But what food that gives to rumour.

At three o'clock I went down to meet the family. They'd a handful of things that'd been in Arthur's pocket when he fell: papers, a new diary for 1973, meetings already pencilled in. I'd take some of the papers — to do with the small shops question, his great campaign to get new corner shops built. The family asked me, because I am a writer, aren't I?, to concoct the memorial for the local paper's death column. For a moment I thought of being original but somehow it wasn't the time. We got some old newspapers and I read out loud what others had put in for theirs, and then we copied down the phrases we liked: "patiently borne" — that's nice — "united with mother and baby", "passed away sudden" — you can't say died. "Never be forgotten", "he left without a last goodbye" — trite? True.

The widow seemed sprightly, but the grandchildren, they weep, the young uncontrollable as we hammer out the arrangements. There will be a lying-in at the under-taker's, and the Tenants' Association will provide pallbearers. Two of us will ride in the family car. How about flowers? Who's going to make them over Christmas? Florists will all be shut, and we've got to have flowers. I tell them I'll see Derek. Our street stewards convener, he's got a grocer's shop with market connections. Leave it to me. The widow insists the family pay for all the notices in the paper, so there's a great reckoning up and sorting out of small change. "He was always straight, Arthur, he'd have wished it — now how much do I owe you if you take the notice to the paper for us?" It's a comfort, oddly, being penny-minded and small change prudent in this storm; but the grandchildren, how they cried. Why are the young closer to death? We have too many wanting to be pallbearers. I suppose we'll have to draw lots. One of the weeping grandchildren leaves the house to walk off into the derelict, and she gets lost. A search party goes out for her, torches in the dark. I leave them — sleep on the train Manchester bound again.

Thursday, 21 December. Straight into the studio this morning without going to my office. We record the commentary, first take. I leave without going to the canteen. Speak to no-one, coffee from a corridor machine and taxi back to the station. Train and sleep. They want the bit on dog racing more quickly. What shall I do about Christmas?

Friday, 22 December. A meeting last night in a room above the local pub. A Labour Party politician said you can't have a tenants' association without a secretary. Call an emergency meeting. I will not. In the upstairs room it's counselling time with three families left holding out on rent strike. Against the Fair Rent increase for council house tenants. We organised a rent strike in the summer, everybody was with us. Say no, mass meetings, lobbies and leaflets. The doubters said — everyone'll pay in the end. They were right. Here are the last three telling me: I would carry on not paying, but it's the wife you see, she worries about eviction so we've got to pay, haven't we? The last three resisters are not lefties at all. They're quiet and determined, puritan proud rather than socialist families. Arthur would have liked them. No boozy talk here, but sober determination not to pay simply because they have no right of appeal against an arbitrary increase. It isn't fair. They're right. We've lost.

Saturday, 23 December. And it goes on and on. Christmas is coming and I haven't got a chance. I'm doing the complaints' bureau down at the shop when the chairman of a new Labour city council committee calls. Can I prepare a report on the need for community facilities for a special meeting the council have for the 28th, that's the day of Arthur's funeral — Christmas is gone. If I do a good report we stand a chance of getting a permanent headquarters. I cancel all the plans I had for seeing my mother and father at Christmas. Tuesday, 26 December. It's been a nice Christmas. John came home unexpectedly in a taxi on Christmas Day from Los Angeles. Friends came round to eat. I slept a lot.

Wednesday, 27 December. On Boxing Day I took the dogs for a walk, to talk to people about Arthur. Today I've been to see him, viewing they call it, at the lying-in at the undertaker's. The rooms were lined with wood like ships. I've come to see Mr Leatherland, I said, and a prim lady through a little hatch in the panelled wood said: "Take a seat for a moment, would you, please."

The undertaker's smelt very nice, a cross between a florist's and a curry shop. Arthur lay in the coffin. You could see the bruises on his face where he fell. He was surprisingly small and still with his eyes closed. I'd never seen him with his eyes closed. I prayed to God, demanding he bring Arthur back, to let his keen eyes open and sort out this Christmas parcel wrangle.

There was a meeting to work out pallbearers. It was surprisingly calm. Derek had organised the wreaths. Sid had six black armbands for all the bearers, the cars had been told to drive slowly through the streets, and the vicar, though a new man, would do the service appropriately. Walking home I said to myself, he's dead, all dead and gone. Let's bury the dead and be done.

Thursday, 28 December. So, the day of the funeral and we gathered in the street. In the cold morning in the only part of the district left that looks the same now as it did when we began seven years ago before the demolition, before the redevelopment. The corporation had wanted this street down, his street, Arthur's street — but he didn't and it stands the same today at his funeral. There were councillors and committee and ordinary folk, each group a little apart from the terraced home of his widow and the bereaved family. All over the district, folk thought he owned that house, so hard he fought to keep his terrace up, but he didn't. He rented it. He was a poor man, though whoever called him poor, would have to face some fury.

Funeral cars were late. Arthur hated being late and I was the last one out of the house. So I turned the key and I put it in my pocket. As the cars took off, I realised I'd probably locked out whoever was going to get the funeral tea. But what should I do? Tap on the window: "Driver, d'you mind overtaking and honking the two front funeral cars, 'cause Trevor and Derek and the widow are up front and they won't realise I've locked the auntie out." When we get back there'll be no funeral tea. Folk stand at derelict street ends with their heads bowed. They come out of pub doors and the last corner shop to see the procession pass. Why have we no graveyard in our new world plan — why do we have to cross the town to this vast deaditorium?

At the municipal cemetery, just as at the doctor, the dentist and the hospital, there was a queue. A traffic jam. After some time an usher waves us forward. We'll carry the coffin, thank you. And on our shoulders, into the chapel, the six of us including — Arthur would have been so pleased — one of the original students, now an architect practising in Liverpool. The service was short and simple. The new vicar did it in an Ulster accent that seemed fitting for funerals. And the usher then had us go forward to carry the coffin out. I got it on the front, on the shoulder of my bad arm, and we walked — it seemed an eternity, my only thought was don't drop the coffin — over gravel and tarmac, rough tufts of grass and paving. Were we going too fast? Whatever, it was a bumpy last journey for Arthur. I don't think he'd have enjoyed being on top of our shoulders.

Ashes to ashes, weeping and then to the cars. Margaret was moved; we went together into the third car. She was about to cry. I wanted to laugh. I don't know why. I had to bite my lip. I could see him, the old buzzard, last time I was at the gardens, pushing his fork and his old gardening hat on his head and a drop on the end of his nose.

"Too soft, Margaret is." I laughed. "No use laughing, I'm telling you. She's too soft. All that sociology. Soft with people who won't go to work. Who won't. People use her and I won't have it."

I put my arm round Margaret in the third car, crushed among the lesser relatives. A kind of third division. I closed my eyes, we hadn't got out of the cemetery gates before the relatives started their cackling.

"I'm glad he died so sudden. I'd like to go that way. Some do linger. D'you remember Uncle Tom with half a lung? Ah and Eric — d'you remember Eric? They took one leg off. He could speak then, with the stump all bagged in salt, but when they took the other off, well. Hasn't she taken it well? She doesn't know what's hit her yet. She doesn't. So sudden. Such a shock but I'd like to go that way myself."

Covering death with waves of bread and butter, tins of salmon and tea. All locked in the house, because the key's in my pocket. We cover the thought of death with prattle. We never stop to think if what the preacher says is true: is there a life after death? Can Arthur see us now? Why did I find it so difficult to pray for his soul? I kept my eyes closed all the twenty minute drive back from the cemetery. Counting where we were by the bumps and turns of the car on the road. I'd hate to be blind. Thinking

244

of Arthur, thinking of problems. Now he's gone we have to soldier on. Business to attend to. Even at the graveside: "Nice to see you at the funeral, Councillor Carroll. About this business of planting trees. It is tree planting year. How's it going? How many will we get?" I should have said it but I didn't. He was there and captive was the boss councillor. Arthur would have done. Always. Any chance, at the end of any old meeting, he'd buttonhole someone to press a pet theme. Corner shops. This deserving old person. That disabled lady. Pressing, persistent and thorough. The back door, the front door, office and home. He'd have done it at his own funeral if he could. I hadn't the courage. He used everything but the telephone. He could never use the telephone. Arthur didn't understand it.

They were all outside the house, waiting for our third car and me with the key. It was true, I had inadvertently locked everyone out, including the auntie who was going to make the tea and had just stood outside, just a moment to watch the procession leave. When she turned to go inside to set table for funeral eats, she found herself locked out by me. "That's the trouble with you," old Arthur would have said: "You mean so well, but you don't understand. Let some things be. You don't think: you won't look."

Licking my wounds

Arthur died, and I faded out as chairman. Quite soon after retiring, I could see the central theme of what I wanted to say. I went to deliver it, first, not to the BBC but to my own people. Every month in an upstairs room above a pub the intelligentsia of the neighbourhood meet at a lunch forum not to make decisions but to listen to a speaker. And I got myself invited to speak. I said: "We have lost the dream we had. I can't yet see how it could have been prevented, but we've done it: thrown the baby out with the bath water. We were a slum rich in life and now we've become a very boring, decent, council house estate." Oh, the audience said, now, come, come, that is not true.

I wish I could find a full set of the notes I made for that speech. I wrote them out and put them so carefully away. But I can't find them. The evening paper reported, but not fully. And the scraps of paper, the early drafts of what became my speech, I don't think I actually said — "We were poor but we were happy," I never said that. I did say we were a slum: I used that word — of shocking houses and filthy drains and couldn't care less landlords but we had a rich and varied social life of pub and church and corner shop and lots of activity. And the nooks and crannies to make more activity. There were no planning regulations. Mixed housing and backyard industry. These have gone. The better-off people, the cream who lived in corner shops and the few who owned their own homes, have gone, for in our new paradise there has been but one builder: the council. Anyone wanting to own a different kind of house has had to move away. We've been topped and tailed. For our scruffy, our eccentric, screwballs and oddballs have also been cleared out. In the new housing units haven't been built in sizes and rents to fit funny families.

Where in this new world we built is the warmth, colour, character and easy community spirit we used to have? We didn't used to need organisation. And in the rush for order and planning, for high housing standards of cleanliness and security we have no place for the ambitious, the principled, the devoted and the odd. There were hundreds of little factories and family workshops, and they've all gone bar a couple of big ones — either retired, bankrupt or moved on to purpose built industrial estates. When we were a slum, people came into the area to buy bread on a Sunday, and to work from Monday to Friday, and down for all kinds of knees-up on a Saturday night. We had life. A speciality that attracted outsiders/tourists into the neighbourhood.

Now we've been redeveloped, no-one comes into the area any more to work, shop, or sing or dance. Only to teach. We're left alone now: up a cultural cul-de-sac. We were the life and the soul of the scrubbers' end of town and like a goodtime girl who's taken to religion, when cleaned up we're deadly prim and boring.

Though our redevelopment has been good — in that we haven't had the worst of the new barbarism inflicted on us — it's not so good for fighting spirit that our new is nice. We fought against motorways carving up the neighbourhood and we won. We fought against having high rise flats, budgie boxes in the sky, and we won. We've got plasterboard rabbit hutches on the ground instead. We're about as poor now as then — in comparison to how rich the rich are — but we have nothing spectacular any more to show that we're poor. And that poverty can have a heart of gold and its own laughter. In our dying days, sociologists came by the minibus-load to point and preach from our plight. They don't come now. We've had our moment. We've been done. We've problems still, but none of the pleasures, none of the little compensations any more. Oh, there are the private pleasures of taking a bath and central heating at home but no public pleasure. Not a pub with a room

247

above for hire. Not a shop selling anything but the necessities of life. No church with a graveyard. We've been insecticised and our germs exterminated, and along with them our butterflies and wasps that stung and bees that made such honey.

In the early days our people didn't want to move away into overspill estates. They said they liked the neighbourliness downtown. Little did we realise when downtown was rebuilt it would be more dead and less neighbourly than the overspill estates. The suburbs is where life is today. We pulled down a nineteenth-century slum and built a twentieth-century ghetto in its place, for the dim, the henpecked and the house proud.

I don't think I said that — "henpecked and house proud" — but it's in my early notes. I certainly said enough to really take some stick for sticking my neck out at that lunch forum. Kangaroo court — I got roasted at the next committee meeting. Some sent me to Coventry. My knuckles rapped. My speech had raised the hackles of decent family people. The Sea Scouts, I think it was, wrote to me with a list of all the activities they do: "We're not dead." I must be out of touch, said the churches, all the work we do. Full of activities — we lay on — if only people would join. It is here for them. The new tenants' leader who took over from me, re-read the report of my speech back to me, as reported in the paper, to a crowded public room. I was embarrassed and had so little defence. It seemed I had kicked and spat at the organisation I had helped to build: that was how they took it.

I could see the point. Licking my wounds I retired back to think. Something was wrong, I could tell by those who befriended my speech: old landlords wrote saying how glad they were someone had said it. I was quite right: the area should never have been pulled down. I never said that. Sweatshop factory owners phoned me up to praise my courage. Their little homes, they were little palaces, weren't they? Inside: little palaces. And adjacent to the place of work: so convenient for them. Tarts and hippies stopped me in the streets to say — "What you said, too true, those days were great; dancing all night long; shebeening; down there was one long party."

People are not statistics, or local colour, copy or units; but folk I know who also know me. And they are vulnerable, sensitive to insult and protective of their own, even against the truth. They want to know the truth — but they are like patients coming round in hospital after a series of serious operations. They say, "How am I, doctor?" half expecting bad news. Quick to make a joke against themselves: "I'm feeling worse now, doctor, than I did. Did you leave the scissors in?" Suspicious of good news: ready to give the lie to any bad reports. What does a doctor tell a patient in such a condition? Does he lie? Knowing that feeling good aids recovery. Or tell the truth as you see it? — which is always to a dreamer like a curate's egg, more often than not, all ifs and buts and percentages of fear as well as hope.

I walked through the scheme today and see quite a few things are the way they are because I had a hand in the decision. I was one of the judges on the garden competition — I do still live a part life there. With me was an expert gardener from the council Parks Department and a factory worker, Mrs Charlesworth, who had lived in the old and now lived in the middle of the new estate. She'd given a most beautiful trophy as a first prize to help people do their gardens and make the whole estate look nice. We had other prizes, there were twenty-four entries. It was a very hot day for judging. And we'd judged about half, front and back gardens, and it was gone three o'clock, after the pubs were shut. We were sweating, trudging uphill, puffing into the newest part of the estate. Contractors dust was still swirling about — when we came upon a large family, sitting in their front, open plan garden. They were sitting on orange boxes, cardboard crates in a dustbowl of a lawn with a dandelion border. The men were in singlets. The women just a brassiere on their tops. The doors and windows were wide open blaring out at full volume — disco disco. There were no curtains at the windows and a lot of laughter. The men had bottles of beer beside their orange boxes and the women cups of — I didn't stay to find out, but the cups had handles broken and lips chipped. The children were barefoot and half naked, all were absolutely filthy, throwing dry mud pies, great clumps and clods of earth at each other and all over the public footpath. The family hadn't entered the garden competition, and seeing us pass by with pads and pencils they must have thought we were from the corporation or social security I dare say, for an obscenity was mouthed at one of us. As soon as we turned the corner we looked at one another. "Well," said Mrs Charlesworth, "did you see that? Isn't that just disgusting? But it's what it's coming to — be as bad as it was before you can say Jack Robinson will this estate the way things are going."

I bit my lip: because that house on the corner was of a design not included in the early stages and specially built later on, with five bedrooms for large families, at our insistence — my insistence. Now large does not necessarily mean dirty. But on a housing estate trying to improve its new image, rather than a terraced street coming down, the large family stands out like a sore thumb, having more room to make pleasure or a nuisance.

There were no plans for large family houses until we, me and the others, jumped up and down, raised such a song and dance to get them that way. To create a mixed community was one of the ideas I was most keen on. Big houses for big families with big troubles. I wonder would it have been better if I'd just let be? Let large families be shifted somewhere else not brand new? Most were. Why not let them all go? Better for the general good I'd not made waves.

I wasn't born there, bred or raised. I'm not a native of what I call my district. And I'm not a family man. I'm a latter day immigrant who freely chose to foist myself on "poor" people, like a Robin Hood, to fire slings and arrows at Aunt Sallies for the gratification of my own principles and my own amusement as much as anybody's good. That's the truth. We'd a lot of fun in those tumbledown days. Hippies playing at being parish priests.

Thanks

To Andre Deutsch Ltd for permission to quote from *The Subterraneans* by Jack Kerouac; and to Tuba Press for permission to reproduce Paul Potts' poem, "On Hugh MacDiarmid's 70th Birthday", from *Instead of a Sonnet.* To Rosemary Goad at Faber, and Neil Tennant for copy editing; to Harry Thompson for typing the final draft, and Margaret Behrman for research into the "Battle for the Slums" chapters.

Various stories and ideas in this book have previously been ventilated and have appeared in a different form and I acknowledge in particular the *Daily Telegraph Magazine* and *Tribune, Anarchy* and *New Left Review, Chase Chat, Resurgence, Nottingham Quarterly* and *Nottingham Topic,* Martin Brian O'Keefe, Granada Television (Denis Mitchell), BBC radio (Michael Mason and Tony Gould).

Thanks to all the people who lent me money, and in other ways kept me alive and have not yet seen a return. Most of all to Mary Lander, to whom I dedicate the book: a gentle lady to whose house in the country I ran for cover in the worst of days. It was always good to know you'd listen when I talked, through my rubbish to the grain of sense: that you wanted the generous instinct to succeed. You were so glad Margaret Thatcher came to power in 1979. That you were is a measure of my generation's failure.

To the next generation — I hope.

Ray Gosling,
London, Nottingham and Manchester:
1979